THE ARRIVAL

THE ARRIVAL

A COMEDY IN TWO ACTS

JOHN WIRTH

Christmas is over and Business is Business.
——*Franklin Pierce Adams*

Business is Busyness.
——*The Attendant*

Lying never did anybody any good.
——*The Husband*

Cast

THE WIFE, a tall, trim woman in her thirties

THE HUSBAND, a moderately overweight man of average height in his forties

THE INFANT, a boy about nine or ten years old

THE ATTENDANT, a middle-aged, tall, stocky man. He successively assumes the roles of porter, hotel front desk clerk, bellhop, and doctor.

THE DIRECTOR, a tall young, very handsome man of athletic build in his twenties

ACT ONE

The Arrival

#

The house lights go down. The stage is lit dimly.

At center stage is an overly large overstuffed sofa. Downstage near the right edge of the stage is a chest-high hotel reception counter facing left, angled somewhat toward the audience. Behind it is a wall with a large pigeonhole compartment. On the counter are papers, registers, ledgers, cards, etc. piled haphazardly and a telephone and a desk call bell. Papers, keys, envelopes, etc. are stuffed haphazardly in the pigeonholes. A railless staircase of seven or eight steps leads up to a closed door in the back wall. To the right upstage is a wooden tennis umpire's chair. It is painted white. It is of exaggerated height, elevating its occupant ten feet or more. A portable phonograph player sits on a shelf attached to one of its arms. Farther right and farther downstage is a clothes tree with jackets, hats and other items hanging on it. One of the items is a doctor's bag, hung on a hook by its handle.

There is an interval.

THE DIRECTOR *steps on stage from the right, upstage from the counter.*
He is exceedingly handsome. His hair is blond. It is a very light blond.
He is dressed all in white. He wears a white dress military uniform. His white trousers are bloused over white combat boots. He wears white gloves. He wears a white service cap. Its bill is white. Its crown is even higher and wider than the crowns of the service caps of the North Koreans. The jacket has epaulets and pockets with scalloped flaps. On one of the breast pockets and on the peak of the service cap is an oversized spread wings insignium. A great many medals, decorations, badges, fourragères, ribbons, braids, and insignia cover the entire front of the jacket from top to bottom. There are too many to fit neatly and so are in some disarray. He carries a baton wedged under an arm.

He steps to the downstage center of the stage and halts facing one section of the audience. He takes a few steps and looks at another section of the audience. He turns

5

around and inspects the stage and props.

There is a blank expression on his face. He appears bored. He looks at his watch.

He turns around and looks at the stage and props. He turns back and faces the audience. He points the baton upward and jerks it upward three or four times as a signal to raise the stage lights. After seven or eight seconds the stage lights brighten. He turns around and observes the effect of this change in the lighting.

He proceeds to inspect the props as a pilot performs a perfunctory inspection of his plane before takeoff.

He walks behind the sofa. He runs his hand along the top edge of one or more of the back cushions. He pushes at a coroner of the sofa to adjusts its position very slightly. He walks back to the front of the sofa. He removes one of the cushions. He runs his hand around the edges of the vacated space as if checking for lost coins. He finds at least one and puts it in his pocket.

He walks to the counter of the front desk. He glances at the disshelved papers. He touches some of them. He picks up a handful. He glances at them. He tosses them back on the counter, some of them falling to the floor. He rings the desk call bell.

He walks to the clothes tree. He picks up a few of the pieces of clothing hanging on it and replaces them. He takes a stethoscope from the hook where it hangs and looks at it and puts it back. He takes the doctor's bag from the hook where it hangs by its handle and looks inside. He puts it back on the hook.

He steps upstage to the umpire's chair. With two hands he takes hold of one of its legs and pushes and pulls at it. He is testing the stability of the very tall structure. He does not produce any great movement of the chair. He climbs halfway up the ladder on the front of the chair. He holds on to the legs and shifts his weight from side to side. He appears satisfied that the chair is stable.

He looks around, noting what remains to inspected. He steps back upstage and climbs the staircase to the door. He opens the door and looks behind it. He observes for a few seconds. He closes the door. He steps down the stairs.

He steps to the right and steps offstage where he stepped on stage..

\#

There is an interval of about fifteen seconds.

The Arrival

At the spot he walked offstage, THE DIRECTOR *steps back on stage.*

He carries a phonograph record in its sleeve and a script. The script is sheets bound sin heavy cardstock. He steps to the umpire's chair. Holding the record and script in one hand, he climbs the ladder on the front of the chair. He sits down, tossing the script on the shelf attached to the chair arm. He places the record beside the phonograph. He removes the lid of the phonograph.

He removes his gloves and places them under an epaulette. He takes his glasses from a pocket, removes them from their case, and puts them one. The thick rims of the glasses are white. He removes the record from the sleeve and puts it on the turntable. He manipulates the phonograph's controls. He lifts the tone arm and inspects the needle. He swipes his finger across the needle and a very loud noise sounds.

He switches on the turntable and lets the needle fall on the record and extremely loud music that seems to shake the theater sounds. He quickly snatches the tone arm from the record. He manipulates the controls. He lets the needle fall on the record and music sounds at a low volume. He lifts the needle. He manipulates the controls. He lets the needle fall and music of an even lower volume sounds. He lifts the needle. He manipulates the controls. He lets the needle fall and music sounds that is loud but not as loud as the first music. He lifts the needle and switches off the turntable.

He picks up the script and fans it and turns to a few random pages, giving them a quick look. He turns to the first page and lays the script open on the shelf.

It becomes apparent early in the course of the play that the script is the script of the play-within-the-play. It becomes apparent that the task THE DIRECTOR *has set himself is to follow the action on stage in the script.*

But THE DIRECTOR*'s actions will convey indifference to this task, boredom with it, and inattention to it. A number of times he will nod off and when he wakes up will have to turn over multiple pages of the script to find his place. He will be distracted from constantly looking at the script and find himself looking absently off into the distance. He will be distracted by lighting and smoking cigarettes, in a long cigarette holder. He will be distracted by inspecting his uniform and picking off foreign matter from it. A couple times he takes off his glasses and cleans them with a white handkerchief. More than once, he will pick up the record sleeve, inspect it closely, and replace it on the shelf. He will clean under his nails with a nailfile and file his nails.*

He will be inconsistent in expressing his displeasure when the actors depart from the script and speak out of character. Sometimes he will object vehemently, sometimes mildly. Sometimes he will not seem to be aware that the actors are not following he script.

#

THE HUSBAND *and The* ATTENDANT *come on stage from the right, upstage from the counter.*

THE HUSBAND *looks at the suitcase. He steps over to it. He looks at it closely. He kicks it. He takes the handle of one with one hand and pulls up on it. The suitcase does not budge. He pulls up with greater force, exerting himself. He succeeds in lifting the suitcase five or six inches off the floor. He abruptly lets go of the handle. Muttering.* Jeez!

At the moment the suitcase strikes the floor, a very loud sound-effects-generated THUD! *sounds. Throughout the play, this thud sounds whenever the suitcase is dropped.*

THE HUSBAND *watches* THE ATTENDANT *as* THE ATTENDANT *leans down to look closely at one of the marks for the sofa on the floor.* THE ATTENDANT *adjusts the position of the sofa very slightly. He takes a cushion from he sofa, fluffs it up, and puts it back.*

THE HUSBAND. *To* THE ATTENDANT. Chad . . .

THE ATTENDANT. *Not looking at him.* Yeah?

THE HUSBAND. You can get the bag . . .

THE ATTENDANT. *As if he did not want to hear what* THE HUSBAND *has said.* What?

THE HUSBAND. The bag. You can get it.

THE ATTENDANT. You can do that.

THE HUSBAND. I did it last show.

THE ATTENDANT. *Still not looking at him. He is looks up at some of the stage lights.* Did you? . . . I don't remember. . . . It's nothing. . . . You do it.

THE HUSBAND. Ah c'mon.

THE ATTENDANT *takes a deep breath and exhales. He crosses his arms over his chest.*

THE HUSBAND. *Hostile.* You know what? I should *make* you.

THE ATTENDANT, *with the meaning "What's that you said?", giving* THE HUSBAND *an out.* What's that?

THE HUSBAND *misconstrues* THE ATTENDANT *to ask "What is it you should make*

8

me do?" Carry the friggin' bag.

THE ATTENDANT. *Dismissive, as if he regards* THE HUSBAND *threatening him as an absurdity. Flatly, quietly.* Ridiculous.

THE HUSBAND. *Hostile.* What's the ridiculous?

THE ATTENDANT. *Flatly, quietly.* I'm bigger than you.

THE HUSBAND *exhales angrily through his clenched teeth. Under his breath as he steps back to the suitcase.* Son of a bi— *(his words trail off).*

THE HUSBAND *steps to the suitcase and grasps the handle with both hands. With great effort he lifts it five or six inches off the floor. He laboriously carries it offstage to the left, stopping once or twice, letting the suitcases drop to the floor, breathing deeply, and shaking his hands as if to relieve cramps in his fingers and hands.*

THE HUSBAND *steps back on stage and approaches* THE ATTENDANT, *repeatedly looking back at* THE DIRECTOR *to see if* THE DIRECTOR *is paying attention to him.* THE DIRECTOR *is occupied making notes in the script and is paying no attention to him.*

THE HUSBAND, *approaching* THE ATTENDANT. *In a flat, business-like tone that gives no indication at all that he has just expressed exasperation with The Attendant.*

THE HUSBAND. Got a question for you. . . . *He puts his hand on* THE ATTENDANT's *far shoulder and glances back again at* THE DIRECTOR. *He draws* THE ATTENDANT *downstage to near the edge of the stage as if to be as far as possible from* THE DIRECTOR *'s hearing.*

THE ATTENDANT. *Offhanded.* Wha? *He answers as if somewhat interested in what* THE HUSBAND *might ask him and allows himself to be guided downstage.*

THE HUSBAND. What's with these bags? Why do they have to be so friggin' heavy?

THE ATTENDANT. *Pulling away from* THE HUSBAND *and grimacing, annoyed that* THE HUSBAND *continues to be preoccupied with the suitcase.* They're supposed to be heavy. He *(indicating* THE DIRECTOR*)* wants them heavy. It's part of the play.

THE HUSBAND. But why are they heavy *really.*

THE ATTENDANT. Well . . . you know . . . it's . . . . you know . . . like for the sake of reality—*realism.*

THE HUSBAND. *Screw* reality.

THE ATTENDANT *shrugs his shoulders, bouncing on his heels and looking out into the*

9

audience.

THE HUSBAND. We could just empty it out. Throw everything in the trash.

THE ATTENDANT. No. He'd know.

THE HUSBAND. This is crazy. Why doesn't he do that?

THE ATTENDANT. *Indifferent.* I don't know. . . . Maybe . . . maybe he doesn't like you.

THE HUSBAND *rolls his eyes.* Ah . . . the guy's crazy.

THE ATTENDANT *steps to the sofa and bends down to check another mark.*

THE HUSBAND *steps to the right and steps off stage where he stepped on stage.*

THE ATTENDANT *steps to the clothes tree. He puts on a porter's jacket. He puts on a porter's cap.*

The porter's cap and jacket are the Pullman porter's dark kepi cap and long, dark jacket.

He steps offstage to the right upstage from the reception desk.

#

There is an interval of about fifteen seconds.

The lights come up full on the downstage, including the reception counter and wall with pigeonholes. The sofa and clothes tree remain dimly lit. THE DIRECTOR *and the umpire's chair are lit with an intermediate intensity.*

There is a pause of about ten seconds.

THE WIFE *steps on stage from the left, walks to the center of the downstage, and halts.*

She is dressed in a plain house dress and a plain calf-length overcoat. In her left hand she carries a large round cloth handbag that is stuffed full. She carries the handbag tight against her abdomen. Until the end of the first act she never moves it from that position.

THE WIFE *turns and looks offstage to the left. Gesturing with her hand to a person offstage.* C'mon. Let's go.

She pauses.

THE WIFE. *Gesturing again.* Come *on.*

THE ATTENDANT (AS PORTER) steps on stage from the right, downstage from the reception desk. He wears the Pullman porter's cap and jacket.

10

The Arrival

THE ATTENDANT (AS PORTER), *stepping across the stage to* THE WIFE. Well. hel-*lo*. THE WIFE *turns and faces him.* As you know from your previous service—*(quickly correcting himself) experience* here, I am the porter. My name is Fred—or, if you prefer, Frankie for short. And you are of course Mrs. . . . uh . . . uh . . .

THE WIFE. Mrs. Sm—

The Attendant (as porter), *interrupting.* No, no, no. Don't say it. I'll think of it in a minute or two. *He pauses briefly.* Cherry. How we doin' today, ma'am?

THE WIFE. Let's not get into that.

THE ATTENDANT (AS PORTER). *Deflated.* Right.

THE WIFE. It's not snowing.

THE ATTENDANT (AS PORTER). *Jumping on her words, rapidly.* No, it's not. No, indeed. Quite right. Right you are. Indeed so. We don't need more snow. *He pauses briefly, as if thinking. More measured.* That is to say, we don't need more snow or *any* snow, as the case may be.

The very loud thump, produced by sound effects, that previously sounded now sounds again, from offstage to the left.

In response, THE WIFE *and* THE ATTENDANT (AS PORTER) *look offstage to the left.*

THE WIFE. *To the person offstage to the left.* C'mon. Hey, let's get going.

THE ATTENDANT (AS PORTER). The person whom you are addressing is your husband, of course . . .

The Wife. You can depend on it.

THE ATTENDANT (AS PORTER). I know him well. I'd know him anywhere. A good man. Sincere. Trustworthy.

Excuse me. Your husband is soliciting my professional services. I'll just see what I can do to him—*(quickly correcting himself) for* him. You just go right ahead and stand there and make yourself comfortable.

He walks rapidly to the left. Beginning to speak before he reaches the left edge of the stage and continuing to speak offstage. Here. Here. Whoa. Let me help you with that, sir. You're bound to drop it again, as weak as you are, sir. Let me keep you from injuring yourself.

The following exchange occurs offstage while THE WIFE *stands listening to it and watching.*

The Arrival

THE HUSBAND. *Annoyed.* Hey, who are you?

THE ATTENDANT (AS PORTER). Well, well, well. Here we all are: Mr. . . . uh . . . the mister and the lovely wife. And me. Well, here we go round again, right?

THE HUSBAND. *Annoyed, becoming angry.* What're you talking about? What're you doing? Get your hand off my luggage.

THE ATTENDANT (AS PORTER). You needn't exercise yourself, although my intentions are both dishonorable and dishonest. Deep down I know that you know I am the porter.

THE HUSBAND. I can do this myself.

THE ATTENDANT (AS PORTER). That's not my perception. Okay. Shall we go?

THE HUSBAND *and* THE ATTENDANT (AS PORTER) *come on stage from the left.*

The two of them are lugging a suitcase together. Their right hands are next to each other on the handle. THE HUSBAND *is behind* THE ATTENDANT (AS PORTER). *They take tiny rapid mincing steps to keep from stepping on each other's feet and bump into each other.* THE HUSBAND *strains and grunts.*

THE ATTENDANT (AS PORTER). Let me do this, sir. I am here to do this. This is my job. This is what they pay me for. This is what *you* pay me for.

THE HUSBAND. *Stern.* Take your hand off my property.

THE ATTENDANT (AS PORTER). Oh my! A defender of private property! Wonderful! that's great! Here we have our own little Adam Smith in our midst! *He twists to his right and with his left hand pats The Husband's right shoulder approvingly. Attaboy!*

THE HUSBAND. No. My name is *John* Sm—

THE ATTENDANT (AS PORTER), *interrupting. Please,* sir. I was being figurative.

THE HUSBAND. *Annoyed.* I don't know you.

THE ATTENDANT (AS PORTER). Aha! *But I know you,* . . . uh . . . Tom? . . . uh . . . Dick? . . . . Harry?—whatever your exact name is. What is it, by the way? You can let go if you would . . .

As you recall—or not recall in your case—besides being the official porter I am the official greeter. So let me greet you. *Greetings! Addressing* THE

WIFE. To the both of you. Or should say to the thr—*(catching himself, speaking the following very rapidly.* No no no, I don't want to go down that route—*decidedly. Slower.* Our corporate greeting is intended, of course, to put you at ease *(he pauses for a moment)* and to throw you off guard.

And *now* what can I do for you—what *else.*

THE HUSBAND *(not in response to* THE ATTENDANT (AS PORTER)*'s question but expressing again his general annoyance with him).* Get lost.

THE ATTENDANT (AS PORTER) *(puzzled, interpreting* THE HUSBAND*'s response to be an answer to his question).* That's not one of the *elses.* Me *get lost?* My sense of direction is infallible. I am drawn in a direct line to the vulnerable.

He pauses. You may let go at any time. You do not get a discount by trying to help me.

For ten seconds or so, the two of them try to pull the suitcase out of the other's hand. They push and pull at each other. Their hands remain tight on the handle. They both stop and breathe deeply from their exertion.

THE ATTENDANT (AS PORTER). I warrant it is not my intention to remain attached to you in this way for the rest of the day. It is my contention that the physics of this configuration bears close scientific scrutiny.

THE HUSBAND. *Annoyed, hostile.* Bug off, bub.

THE ATTENDANT (AS PORTER). We are dual supports of this load. From this it can be logically deduced from physics that you, being embarrassingly physically weak, are—as you have demonstrated a couple minutes ago—incapable of supporting it alone. Therefore, I recommend that you move your feet out of the way of the load when it falls as I am of a mind to terminate my support at any moment.

THE HUSBAND. Fine. Bye. Nice to know a.

THE ATTENDANT (AS PORTER). Five, four, three, two, one, zero, *bingo! He releases his grip on the suitcase.*

THE HUSBAND *instantly grabs the handle of the suitcase with his left hand, replacing* THE ATTENDANT (AS PORTER)*'s right hand. He does not let the suitcase fall. He is determined to keep it from falling by himself.*

THE ATTENDANT (AS PORTER). *Stepping back and observing* THE HUSBAND. *Surprised, nodding, conceding.* Oh dear me. Looked-see. All by hisself.

The Arrival

THE ATTENDANT (AS PORTER) stands looking at THE HUSBAND and
the suitcase for an interval.
THE ATTENDANT (AS PORTER). You can set that down, you know.
THE HUSBAND. No. I don't need to.
THE ATTENDANT (AS PORTER). You don't have to demonstrate a strength
    that is not native to you. We here are your friends, after all.
THE HUSBAND does not respond.
THE ATTENDANT (AS PORTER). I looks to me like you're going to drop it.
THE HUSBAND. Nope.
THE ATTENDANT (AS PORTER) stands looking at THE HUSBAND for ten
seconds or so.
THE ATTENDANT (AS PORTER). You're tired. I can see that. You can hardly
    keep ahold of it.
THE HUSBAND. Wrong.
THE ATTENDANT (AS PORTER) looks at THE HUSBAND and the suitcase. He
    looks around and at his feet, as if thinking. He looks again at THE
    HUSBAND and the suitcase.
    With a sudden start, he points at one of THE HUSBAND's feet and
shouts at the top of his voice. *OH MY GOD! I JUST SAW A MOUSE
CLIMB UP INSIDE YOUR TROUSER LEG!*
THE HUSBAND *does not respond. Matter-of-fact.* I *love* the little guys. I have a pet
    hamster. His name is Bert.
    There is an interval.
THE ATTENDANT (AS PORTER). You don't feel it slipping out of your grip?
THE HUSBAND repositions his hands on the handle, gripping it more tightly.
THE ATTENDANT (AS PORTER) stares at THE HUSBAND for an interval.
THE ATTENDANT (AS PORTER) suddenly points at THE HUSBAND and shouts
    at the top of his voice. *THERE'S A SPIDER IN YOUR HAIR!*
THE HUSBAND *does not respond.* After a pause. Matter-of-fact. I *love* those little
    guys. I have a pet tarantula. His name is Al.
THE ATTENDANT (AS PORTER) *steps this way and that, looking up, with his hands
    on his hips, as if trying to think of another stratagem.*
    *He abruptly dashes from one part of the stage to another screaming FIRE! FIRE!
FIRE! EVERYBODY OUT! FIRE! GET OUT! FIRE! FIRE!*
    None of the other actors react in the least to THE ATTENDANT (AS PORTER)'s

14

outburst. When THE ATTENDANT (AS PORTER) *sees this as he dashes around, he ceases shouting and pulls up near* THE HUSBAND.

THE HUSBAND. *Out of character. Confronting* THE ATTENDANT (AS PORTER), *facing him at close range.* I don't know whether you realize but Mr. White-Guy here (*indicating* THE DIRECTOR) has just had you commit a crime. If there isn't a fire its illegal to yell "fire" in a theater.

THE ATTENDANT (AS PORTER). *Out of character.* Correcting him—"in a *crowded* theater." *He makes a show of looking around at the audience.* Not crowded.

He pauses, looking down at THE HUSBAND*'s hands on the handle of the* suitcase. It appears to me that your attachment to your luggage is very strong. It am not sure whether this trait of your character is an admirable one or not.

In any case . . . *He takes a paper from a pocket of his jacket and holds I out to* THE HUSBAND.

THE HUSBAND. What's that?

THE ATTENDANT (AS PORTER). My bill.

THE HUSBAND. *Panicked. Shrieks. EEEEEEEEEEK! He recoils violently, letting go of the suitcase and inadvertently propelling it away from his body, and it falls on* THE ATTENDANT (AS PORTER)*'s feet.*

The paper falls out of THE ATTENDANT (AS PORTER)*'s hand and drops to the* floor.

THE ATTENDANT (AS PORTER). *Matter-of-fact, not expressing any pain, while pulling his feet from under the suitcase.* Oooooooo. Look at that. Right on my piggies. That's an ouch situation. It is to be assumed that at least one of my biggie piggies has been crushed. *He proceeds without pause, rapidly.* Any medical expenses relevant and irrelevant to this horrific incident will be appendixed to already-incurred charges. *Realizing he has said "appendix."* Oh . . . yeah, sure, *appendix.* . . . Including a charge for an appendix removal. *He thinks for a second.* And including a charge for a tonsils removal (*he pauses briefly)* and let's throw in a circumcision.

THE HUSBAND. I am not responsible. I had to sneeze.

THE ATTENDANT (AS PORTER). Also included of course will be much more than generous compensation for pain and suffering. It seems apparent that I am likely suffering great pain, and suffering great suffering. *He lifts a foot from the floor and shakes it gently.* Indeed, apparently there is perhaps a hint of some unaccustomed sensation coming from there or a nearby area. *He lowers the foot to the floor.* The price for this violation of my body will be exorbitant.

To THE HUSBAND. And I suppose you were about to say that it never happened.

THE HUSBAND. *Matter-of-fact.* No. *After a short pause, as if he thinks of something he wants to say.* But I will if it will make you unhappy. It never happened.

THE ATTENDANT (AS PORTER). Mr. . . . *(he pauses for a moment)* forgive me if I've forgotten your name for a moment—can I be a little personal with you?

THE HUSBAND. *Quickly. Positive.* No.

THE ATTENDANT (AS PORTER). You, by the evidence we see in front of us, have an active sexual side but, as I know you well, I suspect—I *know*—that you also have a strong spiritual side. Is that not correct?

THE HUSBAND. *He is surprised and puzzled by this question. He considers for a few seconds. Tentative.* Maybe.

THE ATTENDANT (AS PORTER) *delivers his spiel by rote and very rapidly.* Now then, Mr. [*he clears his throat to obscure the fact that he has forgotten* THE HUSBAND's *name*], people will tell you that the whereabouts are unknown of the Golden Tablet unearthed at Podunk, New York, from the bank of Taughanook Creek. This is false. The Golden Tablet is in an undisclosed location known only to the members of a secret society whose name is The Society of the Secreted. Every month The Society of the Secreted publishes a newsletter disclosing a never-before-published section of the Tablet, newly translated from the Middle English. . . . This coveted item is printed on acid-free paper. . . . And it comes with a crossword puzzle.

THE HUSBAND. *Realizing that he is the object of a sales pitch.* No, I don't think so.

THE ATTENDANT (AS PORTER). The Ten Commandments is a mere single-page outline. You know what gold leaf is. Each page of The Golden Tablet is a gold leaf. The Golden Tablet consists of hundreds of gold leaves—

pages—of specific and detailed text encompassing thousands of topics.

In fact, Section One of the Golden Tablet, which consists of forty-seven pages, is an index.

To recap, The Ten Commandments are mere talking buttons of a general nature in number a mere decade—not to even mention the possible etymological connection between the words "decade" and "decadence." Moses has left us with few and fuzzy commandments whereas The Golden Tablet's universality and specificity assures you that no part of your life will go uncommanded.

The MSRP is twenty-four ninety-five per issue, which I challenge you to contend is not ridiculously low considering the extraordinary value of this product. However—and this is accordance with an agreement with the Society that I insisted upon—I am empowered to award a discount of five dollars to a person whom I judge to be spiritually worthy, *(placing a hand on The* HUSBAND*'s shoulder and giving it a quick congratulatory shake)* which I deem you to be. *He pauses for a moment, smiling.*

Abruptly resuming his spiel, rubbing his hands together. But there's more. I am prepared to enter into an agreement with you—a private agreement between just you and me—under which I will remit to you one dollar and fifty-five cents of my commission of fifteen per cent or three dollars and twenty-five cents. In other words, you will receive each month more than half of my commission, resulting in the unbelievable arrangement whereby you will actually be making more money than me in this deal.

THE HUSBAND. *Meek.* No, I'd rather not. . . .

THE ATTENDANT (AS PORTER). I'll set that right up for you, Mr. *(he clears his throat)*. You can expect to receive your first issue in between seventy-nine and a hundred thirty-four business days.

There is a long pause.

THE ATTENDANT (AS PORTER), *as if uncomfortable with the long silence, clasping his hands behind his back, twisting from side to side, and looking up and around into the distance.* Ummm. . . . You like magic, sir? I can sell you magic tricks. I *love* magic tricks. I can make your money disappear.

There is another long interval.

THE ATTENDANT (AS PORTER). I now abandon you. I will be servicing a
customer at our VIP entrance. A man—an *extremely* wealthy man, I will
add needlessly—will be granted an emergency admission to our Nelson
A. Rockefeller Pavilion. Our Nelson A. Rockefeller Pavilion, a
nationally top-ranked facility, is one among a chain of—needless to
say—a great many Nelson A. Rockefeller Pavilions spread all across our
great broad wonderful country, each featuring a coronary care unit
specializing in the treatment of the heart attack precipitated by a
stressful situation.

THE ATTENDANT (AS PORTER) *walks swiftly offstage to the right, downstage*
from the counter.

THE HUSBAND. Well, we won't have to see any more of that jackass. Trying
to horn in on the luggage like that . . .

THE WIFE. *To provoke* THE HUSBAND. *Sarcastic.* Last time you were *so generous*
to him. He even wrote you a thank-you note, remember? Enclosing a
nickel, saying you had overpaid.

THE HUSBAND. *Incensed, with exaggerated anger, shouting. THERE WAS NO*
LAST TIME.! I WAS NOT GENEROUS! I AM NEVER
GENEROUS! I HAVEN'T BEEN A DAY I N MY LIFE!

3

THE WIFE. *Indicates the suitcase.* Let's not fumble the ball in the middle of the
field . . .

THE HUSBAND. *Vexed.* All right. *You* carry them.

THE WIFE. We've gone round on this many times. I can't. Not in my
condition.

THE HUSBAND. *Angry.* If you're not in condition you should exercise! . . . *He*
reluctantly picks up the suitcase with both hands. He strains to keep it off the floor.
My God! What have you got in these?

THE WIFE. Oh, nothing at all, not a thing. They're completely empty. . . . I
only put a few little things in them, nothing worth mentioning. THE

HUSBAND'S *grip loosens and the bag slips lower.* . . . What I need to be comfortable, several things. *The bag slips lower.* Some extra things, a good many things. *The bags slip lower.* Everything I own. *The bag slips from the husband's grasp.*

As the bag hits the floor, the very loud sound-effects thud sounds.

THE HUSBAND begins to walk to the left.

THE WIFE. Where are you going?

THE HUSBAND turns and looks at her. Oh. I didn't see you there. Hi. And
    you are . . . ?

THE WIFE. *Matter-of-fact.* Your wife.

THE HUSBAND. Oh, sorry. I didn't recognize you. My glasses got smeared.

THE WIFE. I am obliged to point out that the fact of the matter is that you
    are not wearing glasses.

THE HUSBAND. Exactly. And how can I see you without my glasses?

He looks around. He looks at the suitcase. You know, somehow I got stuck
with this suitcase . . . I'm not just sure where it's supposed to be going to—I
guess this way *(indicating with his thumb the direction to the right-hand edge of the
stage). He pauses as if thinking. Speaking quickly as if an idea has suddenly occurred to
him.* Is it *yours?*

THE WIFE. Yes.

THE HUSBAND. Well, then, why don't you just grab it and . . . uh . . .

*There is an interval. The Wife does not react in any way to what he has said to
her—her way of conveying to him the message, "You know very well I can't lift anything
heavy in my condition."*

THE HUSBAND *shrugs.*

*He steps to the suitcase. He rolls it to the right. He rolls it end-over-end on its edges
one or two revolutions.*

THE HUSBAND. I don't know about you but I'm ready for a break. He
sits down on one corner of the suitcase. THE WIFE sits down on the other
corner.

THE HUSBAND *suddenly jumps up.* Maybe I can find a place where I can
grab us a couple Dr. Peppers. . . .

THE WIFE. *Commanding.* Sit down.

THE HUSBAND *sits back down on the corner of the suitcase.*
There is a long interval.

The Arrival

THE HUSBAND. *To* The Wife, *out of character.* Not much happens in this play, does it?

THE WIFE *shrugs and grimaces in a gesture that conveys,* "Maybe yes, maybe no."

There is another long interval.

The Wife. Time *is* a constraint . . . .

The Husband glances back over his shoulder at The Director, as if to see if The Director is watching them. The Director is smoking and appears sleepy. The Husband extends his hand to The Wife. To The Wife, indicating The Director with his thumb. He's not watching. The Wife stands up and approaches him. To The Wife. "Let's get over there . . . " He takes her by the elbow and draws her downstage as if to be out of the range of The Director's hearing.

THE HUSBAND *again glances back over his shoulder at The Director.*

THE HUSBAND. Again i*ndicating* THE DIRECTOR *with his thumb.* This director guy here . . . . *They turn and look at* THE DIRECTOR. *They turn back.* Who is he . . . exactly?

THE WIFE. Exactly? . . . I don't know.

THE HUSBAND. He doesn't look like much, does he?

THE WIFE. He looks all right to me. He's handsome.

THE HUSBAND. "Handsome"? Are you kidding me? . . He's what they call pretty, but he ain't handsome. *Confiding.* I'll tell you something: I think the guy's a fag or a . . . a defective . . . or something like that. If you ask me, he's not right somehow— *or somewhere.*
They turn and look at THE DIRECTOR. *They turn back.*

THE HUSBAND. Look at them glory clothes he's got on, will you? Tell me there ain't something queer about a guy that'd wear *that.*

THE WIFE. He *is* queer about *white,* isn't he?

THE HUSBAND. *Glumly.* The goddam queers have taken over this here theater business.

THE WIFE: *Tentatively.* Well . . . *After a few seconds' thought. Conceding the point.* Yes. *After another pause, making a point.* Just like the capitalists have taken over the *business* business.

THE HUSBAND *and* THE WIFE *turn and look at* THE DIRECTOR.

THE HUSBAND. *With his hand on his hip, looking at* THE DIRECTOR *quizzically.*

20

I don't know . . . *Considering*. What d'ya think? . . . with that uniform . . .
   maybe he's in the National Guard.
THE WIFE. *Giving the three answers quickly and firmly*. He's a Good Humor ice
   cream truck operator. THE HUSBAND *grimaces dismissively*. He's your
   guardian angel. THE HUSBAND *again grimaces dismissively*. He's a sanitary
   engineer. THE HUSBAND *again grimaces dismissively*.
   THE HUSBAND *and* THE WIFE *turn away turn from* THE DIRECTOR.
THE HUSBAND *cocks his head towards* THE DIRECTOR. He wrote this thing too,
   you know.
THE WIFE. Somebody had to write it.
THE HUSBAND. Believe me, sister, nobody had to write *this* play.
THE WIFE. *Exasperated. Rolls her eyes.*
THE HUSBAND. Well, it's him all right, and don't you think he ain't proud of
   it. He plays the music on that there record player and he's got his little
   part to play like he was an actor. That makes him an actor and the
   writer and the director and the sound-effects man and so he figures he's
   one of them all-around multiple geniuses.
THE WIFE. Right. He's a regular Chaplin.
THE HUSBAND. Chaplain? . . . You mean the guy's a *priest* besides?
THE WIFE. *Dismissing what he says with a wave of her hand.*
      I'd say he *is* pretty smart.
THE HUSBAND, *Scoffing*. Hah! So does he! There ain't no mistake about
   that: you take his word for it and he's the smartest guy since A. Einstein
   him. I guess he figures he's just about God himself.
THE WIFE. God? I'm skeptical.
The Husband. What do you know? You wouldn't know God if you saw him.
The Wife. *You* wouldn't know Mickey Rooney if you saw him.
      They again turn and look at THE DIRECTOR. *They turn back.*
THE HUSBAND. Yeah. . . . And *mean!* I seen some all-American stinkers in
   my time but this guy has got 'em all beat to hell. You can't tell him
   beans about anything.
THE WIFE. But he's *rich* . . .
THE HUSBAND. He's *gotta* be filthy rich from someplace. He hasn't got a
   regular job. He just sits around on his butt all day writing plays.
THE WIFE. Okay, he's on welfare.

THE HUSBAND. Naw. When he's done writing a play he produces it himself, with him being his own angel. I know one thing, though: he won't get rich off of this play. This play is one of those modern plays that makes no sense, so he won't make a dime off it.

THE WIFE. *Thinking.* Mmmmmmmm. . . . Does that follow? . . . Where's this fellow from?

THE HUSBAND. You got me there. . . . I heard somebody say something about way Upstate—

THE WIFE. *Quickly, automatically at hearing the word "upstate." Flatly.* Yonkers.

THE HUSBAND. No, I don't think . . . . No, further up.

THE WIFE. Syracuse? . . . The Shubert brothers were from Syracuse.

THE HUSBAND *and* THE WIFE turn and *look at* THE DIRECTOR.

THE HUSBAND. *Sarcastically.* Does he look like a Shubert brother?

THE WIFE. The short one or the tall one?

THE DIRECTOR *points his baton upward at the lights on himself and the umpire's chair. He moves it upward in a pumping motion as a signal to bring those lights up more.*

THE WIFE. What does that mean?—Watertown?

THE HUSBAND. *A shocking thought occurs to him. With exaggerated alarm.* GOD, YOU DON'T THINK HE'S A *CANADIAN,* DO YOU?
The lights on The Director and the umpire's go up more.

THE WIFE. Nobody knows where he's from and he's so *famous?*

THE HUSBAND. Who said?

THE WIFE. Well . . . you're always hearing his name spoken. . . .

THE HUSBAND *Scoffing.* If he's such a famous guy, show me his celebrity profile in *Time* magazine.

THE WIFE. I don't read *Time* magazine.

THE HUSBAND. *Scoffing.* You don't read *Time* magazine? Hah! Somebody that doesn't read *TIME* MAGAZINE (*pronouncing these two words with wildly exaggerated vehemence*) probably doesn't read *anything!* Do you read the fortunes in fortune cookies?

THE WIFE, *with exaggerated sarcasm.* I read only the Bible. *Quickly thinking of something else she wants to say.* And his celebrity profile isn't in that. *Quickly reconsidering, turning her head with a questioning look on her face.* Or— (*leaving unsaid the "is it?"*

The Arrival

They look at THE DIRECTOR.

THE HUSBAND *and* THE WIFE *step to the suitcase and sit down on it as before.*

THE WIFE. This suitcase isn't self-propelled.

THE HUSBAND stands up. It's the Dr. Pepper. I have to go. I think the City put in a place in about two blocks from here. Or maybe only five blocks.

THE WIFE. *Flatly. Pointing offstage to the left.* There's a bush over there.

THE HUSBAND. Where? There's no bush there.

THE WIFE. Pointing. *There.*

THE HUSBAND. Isn't that magnolia?

The Wife. Perhaps.

The Husband. I don't know . . . a magnolia . . . I might kill it.

THE WIFE. *Pointing again. There.*

THE HUSBAND. I'll probably get lost.

THE WIFE. I wouldn't recommend it.

The Husband walks offstage to the left.

There is a long interval of about thirty seconds.

The Husband appears at the left edge of the stage. His clothes are now in much greater disarray and his hair is mussed. He sways and staggers, apparently barely able to stay standing. He steps haltingly, with his arms stretched out in front of him as if he were blind. Help! Woe is me! Help.

The Wife pays no attention to him, not turning to look at him.

The Husband. Help! I been assaulted! Help me somebody! His leg hits the corner and he stumbles, almost losing his balance and falling. He bends down feels for the suitcase, apparently determining that it is the corner of the suitcase by feel. He sits down on the corner.

The Husband. Is there somebody there? I can't see or hear. I been concussed. I'm discombobulated. Help me!

The Wife. *Matter-of-fact, still not looking at him.* Okay, tell me your version.

The Husband. Did someone say something? I can't hear. I can't see. Is there someone there. Is that a man or a woman? Are you a man or a woman? What are you?

The Wife. Flatly. I'm not a llama.

The Husband. Did somebody say something? Did somebody say "llama." Is there a llama there? Reaching out blindly in front of him as if to discover what is there. There is a llama there? Where is the llama?

The Wife. Emphatically. *No llama.*

The Husband. *With exaggerated anger and vehemence. I DIDN'T SAY THERE WAS! DID I SAY THERE WAS?! DID I SAY THERE WAS A LLAMA?!*

The Husband *(abruptly calm).* I'm beginning to see and hear a little better. I'm beginning to make you out. You remind me of someone I know.

The Wife. Yeah. I know. Your wife.

The Husband. How did you know?

The is an interval of a few seconds.

The Wife. Your version. Your fabrication . . .

The Husband. I was assaulted by a little old lady who said I was trying to kill the magnolia.

Rubbing his chin. Quite a right, that ol' hag has. . . . She tried to kill me and I was very seriously injured. I can hardly walk, let alone fiddle with suitcases.

THE WIFE. It'll work out just fine. At the same time I'm admitted, you can go right there to the ER.

The Husband, *shouting. Not at all! Calm.* Nope. No ER for me. I'm going to depend on some of that kindness of strangers. It's cheaper.

THE WIFE. Lately I have not encountered that many strangers with great stores of kindness.

THE HUSBAND. In that case, my condition will improve rapidly by itself.

There is an interval of ten seconds or so.

THE HUSBAND. Sorry I didn't recognize you at first. Understandable in my condition. You're so much shorter when you're sitting down. And I had no idea you'd be *here.*

You know, confidentially, I think we're in the wrong place and going to the wrong place.

THE WIFE. I was to wait for you right here, where you left me . . . dropped me.

THE HUSBAND. "Dropped" you? *He looks up at a point high above her head. He looks down at her.* Were you hurt?

THE WIFE. You *drove* me here in the car and dropped me *off.*

THE HUSBAND. Did I?

THE WIFE. You don't remember anything from one minute to the next, do you?

THE HUSBAND. Not when it has anything to do with something as unpleasant as this.

THE WIFE. The you *parked* the car and walked *back*.

THE HUSBAND. Walked?

THE WIFE. Back. Walked back. You walked back.

THE HUSBAND, Did I?

THE WIFE. *Exasperated. Explaining.* You walked back. You parked the care where you parked the car and you walked back from that place to this place, here, where you'd already dropped me.

THE HUSBAND. Did I?

THE WIFE. You did.

THE HUSBAND. No, I didn't: I took a taxi.

Explaining. There wasn't any place to park within ten miles of here.

THE WIFE. Ten miles? But our house is only *five* miles from here.

THE HUSBAND. *Snapping his fingers as if he realizes he has made a mistake.* Ah! That's right! I could've parked in our *garage*. . . . Oh, well, it's all right. The taxi ride didn't cost me much: I didn't tip the driver. *He shrugs his shoulders. Conceding.* Oh, he was a little mad about it: he called me a politician and spit at me. But I dodged it. . . . I don't know. . . . I think if I was you I'd have left a note on the sidewalk and gone on without me. . . . You'd be further along now.

THE WIFE. I can't carry the bag.

THE HUSBAND. Why not?

THE WIFE. I'm carrying all I can carry already.

THE HUSBAND *looks at her quizzically for a few seconds.* What's that supposed to mean?

THE WIFE *is silent.*

There is an interval.

THE WIFE. It's taking *too* long.

THE HUSBAND. It's not taking us long. It's not as if there was any reason to be in a hurry, of course.

THE WIFE. *Flatly.* There just may be a reason.

THE HUSBAND. I could take us *years* . . . *two* years . . . *three* years . . *five* years . . .

THE WIFE. *Looking at her watch. Sarcastically.* Twenty-five years.

The Arrival

THE HUSBAND. What I mean is: what's the rush?

THE WIFE. You know.

THE HUSBAND. I certainly do *not* know. . . . I really don't *want* to know, to tell you the truth about it. There isn't any rush, is there?

THE WIFE. There may be.

THE HUSBAND *frowns and shakes his head. He puts his finger in his ear and shakes his hand as if he suspects something is wrong with his hearing.* Did you say there *may be?*

THE WIFE. *Firmly.* You heard me.

THE HUSBAND. *In an earnest tone.* No. Really. Honest. I didn't hear you.

THE WIFE. *With mock concern.* You know, I *have* noticed within the last twenty years or so that you sometimes *do* have a little bit of trouble with your hearing.

THE HUSBAND. *Quickly.* Only when I want to. *Explaining.* It's an old Korean War injury. . . . *Correcting himself.* No, that's not right—I wasn't in the Korean War. *Thinking. Half to himself.* Some other war . . . Let me think . . . Afghanistan War. . . . no, that doesn't sound right . . . Vietnam War . . . no, not that one . . . The Kuwait War . . . no . . . The First Iraq War—

THE WIFE. *Correcting him.* The First Iraq War *was* the Kuwait War.

THE HUSBAND. Really? Neither one rings a bell. *Thinking.* Ummm . . . *Suddenly thinks of something.* The *Grenada War*—that sounds like the right one. As I was saying, it's an old Grenada War injury. You see, I was at the command post. Suddenly there was this terrific explosion: what happened was I stumbled and stepped on the toe of the general's boot and he blew his top. He screamed dirty words right in my ear. *He puts his finger in his ear and shakes his hand.* I think he broke the drum.

THE WIFE. *After an interval, flatly.* Needless to say, you were never in the Grenada War.

THE HUSBAND. *Flatly, wryly.* Needless to say, I was never injured, either. *There is another pause. Deliberatively.* I really can't *understand* why there'd be a rush.

THE WIFE. Your *understanding* has been a little rusty, too. *She considers for a moment. Correcting herself.* Your understanding *never was* too hot.

The Arrival

There is an interval.

THE WIFE. Come on. Let's go. Pick up the bag.

THE HUSBAND. Quiet.

THE WIFE. You could at least be civil.

THE HUSBAND. I'd rather be a successful businessman.

THE WIFE. You're not a successful businessman. You're only a Second Deputy Assistant Manager of Administrative Services—

THE HUSBAND. Well, I may be on my way to First Deputy Assistant Manager, if you'd care to know.

THE WIFE. —at a department store. And it isn't even a *leading* department store.

THE HUSBAND. *Abruptly very angry.* Is that *my* fault! I don't run it! I'm only a Second Deputy! *Abruptly calm.* And besides that, we work under a handicap: the president of the company isn't all there *(he taps his head with his finger)* up here: he had a TIA and lost his business sense. *Very angry again. And besides that, we are too leading! All the newspaper ads say were leading! Don't ever say we're not leading!*

There is an interval.

THE WIFE. *Standing up.* All right. Let's go.

THE HUSBAND. Take it easy. . . . No hurry. . . . I mean, it's not as if we're in a rush . . . it's not as if . . . it's not as if we were going someplace and had to *arrive* at a certain time. . . . *Carelessly.* I mean, it's not as if you were about to have a baby and I was taking you to the hospital. *He chuckles at the idea. He abruptly assumes a shocked expression. He starts and sits stock still, his gestures frozen. There is a pause. He claps his hands to his ears and grimaces as if in pain. Distracted, he gradually composes himself as he speaks. OH! YOU DIDN'T HEAR THAT! PAY NO ATTENTION! I DIDN'T MEAN THAT! What? It was an accident. I didn't say it. Who says I said it? I never, never, never, never said it.* It never happened. I didn't say anything. Nobody said anything. It's been completely quiet around here for quite a while.

THE WIFE. *Very calmly.* My goodness. . . . Quite the temperamental temperament. . . . What's the problem—nerves? . . . stomach? . . . endocrines? *She pauses at length. Very slowly.* Said what? Oh, you mean, that I'm about to have a baby and you're taking me to the hospital. Yes,

27

that may be true.

THE HUSBAND *starts violently and claps his hands to his ears. Shouting.* I DIDN'T
HEAR THAT! YOU DIDN'T SAY THAT! YOU NEVER EVEN
OPENED YOU LOUD MOUTH!

THE WIFE. *Very calmly.* Oh my, oh my, listen to you. . . . There's no reason to
get excited. I just said I may be about to have a baby—

THE HUSBAND *claps his hands over his ears. Don't say that word! I can't stand to hear
that word! It makes me sick! He clutches his abdomen and grimaces.*

THE WIFE. *Very calmly.* It does?

THE HUSBAND. Yes!

THE WIFE. *Very calmly.* Oh? And why does it make you sick?

THE HUSBAND. Because I don't want to *think* about it!

THE WIFE. Oh? And why don't you want to think about it?

THE HUSBAND. *Bellowing.* BECAUSE IT'S GOING TO COST ME
MONEY!, THAT'S WHY!

THE WIFE. *After a pause. Softly, mischievously.* Baby, baby, baby, baby, baby—

THE HUSBAND *frantically claps his hands over his ears again. Shut up! Shut up! Stop
it! Don't say that! Quiet! Quiet! There is a pause. He abruptly recovers his
composure and takes his hands from his ears.*

THE WIFE. *Calmly.* You *do* have a problem there. . . . Well, that was fun. But
the fact probably remains that I may be about to have a—

THE HUSBAND *claps his hands over his ears. He pauses. He warily takes his hands
from his ears.*

THE WIFE. That I may be about to have a—

THE HUSBAND *holds his hands ready to clap them over his ears.*

THE WIFE. To have . . . *(she shrugs her shoulders)* an *object.*

THE HUSBAND *abruptly becomes calm.*

THE HUSBAND. *Matter-of-fact.* It's impossible. You can't.

THE WIFE. Maybe I can.

THE HUSBAND. *Still matter-of-fact.* You *can't!* He quickly takes out his wallet, opens
it and shows it to her. Look at that. It's empty. Completely empty. *He puts
his wallet back in his pocket. He takes out a sheaf of papers.* Look. See these.
Bills, bills, bills. All unpaid bills. Thousands of 'em. *He tears them to pieces
and scatters them. He takes out a small accounts booklet. He opens it and points at
a page.* And look at this. This is the modest family budget. Look. See

here. Red, red, red. All the balances are red. Now tell me where am I going to get the money to pay for an . . . an object? *He tosses the accounts booklet away.*

THE WIFE *shrugs her shoulders.* THE HUSBAND *glares are her.* Beg? . . . . Borrow? . . . Steal? . . . *She considers.* What about bribery? . . . That's legal in America.

THE HUSBAND. *Positive.* That proves it. We can't afford it. It's absolutely impossible for you to have an object. You are *not* going to have an object.

There is an interval.

#

THE INFANT *walks on stage from the right, downstage from the counter. He walks swiftly and purposefully to The Husband and The Wife. He is naked.*

THE HUSBAND *looks at* THE INFANT. *He takes* THE WIFE *'s hand* and pulls her to THE INFANT. To THE WIFE. Here. Come here. *They stand beside* THE INFANT, *looking down at him.* Is this the particular object you say you may have to have?

THE WIFE. *Flatly.* No.

THE HUSBAND. *Quizzical. No?*

THE WIFE. *Definite.* No. *She pauses.* But it's a reasonable facsimile.

THE HUSBAND. *Scoffs.* Why you don't have to have *this* thing, do you?

THE WIFE. Why not? What's wrong with him?

THE HUSBAND. Don't you see? It's a shoddy product. It's as weak as a kitten. . . . It's as ugly as a monkey. . . . It's as dumb as a donkey.

THE WIFE. I don't see it that way.

THE HUSBAND. Look how small it is.

THE WIFE. One size fits all.

THE HUSBAND. And look at that face. It's crooked.

THE WIFE. He's sneering back at you.

THE HUSBAND. And look at that skinny little arm. *He reaches out to take* THE INFANT's *arm.* THE INFANT *shrinks away from him.* Look at that. It's got a bad character, it's a coward: it won't let me twist its arm.

29

THE WIFE. Of sound mind.

THE HUSBAND *suddenly lunges at* THE INFANT *Here!* THE INFANT *evades him.*

THE WIFE. And good reactions.

The Infant walks swiftly and purposefully offstage to the right.

THE HUSBAND. *Coaxing.* Come on. You've changed your mind about maybe having to have an object, haven't you?

THE WIFE. No. I'm a woman. A woman only changes her mind in very dire and deadly emergencies.

THE HUSBAND. *This* is *a very dire and deadly emergency!* This could cost me my life . . . *(he pauses)* savings!

4

THE WIFE. Pick up the bag..

THE HUSBAND *looks offstage to the left.* Excuse me, dearie, I see there's a newsboy across the street. I'll get a paper. *He takes a few steps to the left. He suddenly halts. He turns and faces* THE WIFE. *He speaks as if* THE WIFE *has said something to him.* You say you think that I'm lying and that I'm not going to get a newspaper at all? You think that I'll run off and abandon you and leave you to face it all by yourself, alone? Well, believe me, dearie, nothing could be further from my mind. *He pauses.* I'm going. *He takes a step. He pauses again.* Good-by. *He bolts and goes offstage to the right in a dead run.*

THE WIFE *walks swiftly off stage after him.*

> *There is an interval.*

They come on stage from the left. THE WIFE *draws* THE HUSBAND *after her by his sleeve.*

THE HUSBAND. How did you catch me? I had two blocks on you.

THE WIFE. I headed you off.

THE HUSBAND. You headed me off? Where?

THE WIFE. At the overpass.

> Well, I guess if you're going to start trying to cruelly abandon me—are you going to try to cruelly abandon me again?

THE HUSBAND. I don't know any reason why not.

THE WIFE. Then you'd better give me the keys to the car. . . . Don't tell me you lost them.

THE HUSBAND. I lost them. *He hands her the keys.*

THE WIFE. Where did you park after you left me off? Don't tell me you forgot.

THE HUSBAND. I for—no, I remember. *Positive.* Harry's Parking Lot. *Uncertain.* Or was it Gary's. Larry's? Barry's? Perry's? Jerry's? Terry's? Kerry's? Mary's?—that's it. Mary's Parking Lot. Saint Mary's. It's next to the baptistry.

THE WIFE *smiles mischievously.* Baptistry . . . Baptistry . . . *Baby.* THE HUSBAND *clutches his abdomen, screws up his face and groans.* You should be more careful in what you say. The association of ideas can sometimes be quite painful.

There is a pause.

THE HUSBAND *abruptly claps his hands together with a show of enthusiasm.* Well now! I tell you what I'll do! How would you like to go to Asbury Park? I'll take you to Asbury Park. Come on, let's go to Asbury Park.

THE WIFE. *Flatly.* Why?

THE HUSBAND. Well, there's all kinds of reasons. For one thing, of course, why not? For another thing, it would definitely be more fun than going in *there. He points to the right.* THE WIFE *looks at him. She says nothing. Coaxing.* What if I said it would be cheaper? *She says nothing.* Or Ocean City. I'll take you to Ocean City. *She says nothing.* What've you got against Ocean City, anyway? *He pauses.* Come on, be reasonable. What did Ocean City ever do to you?

THE WIFE. Come on. Pick up the bag.

THE HUSBAND *reluctantly and with difficulty picks up the suitcase. He carries it with difficulty a short distance to the right, halts, and holds it off the floor* Now you carry it. It's *(pointing to her) your* bag, you know.

THE WIFE. And . . . *(pointing to herself)* I . . . am . . . *(pointing to him) your* . . . *wife.*

THE HUSBAND. *Puzzled.* You want me to carry *you,* too?

He suitcase slips out of his hand.

The very loud sound-effects thud sounds as it hits the floor.

The Wife points to the suitcase, points to him, and points to the right.

He picks up the bag and begins carrying it downstage instead of to the right.

THE WIFE. Stop! *She points to the right.*

THE HUSBAND *halts and turns and looks behind him at her.* Oh. There you are. Why don't you keep up with me? . . . *Abruptly outraged. And you dropped the bag! Abruptly calm.* Hey, be careful of that thing. It's made out of top grain leatherette, you know.

THE WIFE. *Still pointing towards the right. Flatly, pronouncing each work separately.* This. Way.

THE HUSBAND *exclaims and shakes his head in exasperation. He carries the suitcase to* THE WIFE *and sets it down He sits down on a corner of the suitcase..*
    There is an interval.

THE HUSBAND. Or Atlantic City. How would you like to go to Atlantic City? THE WIFE *says nothing.* I don't see how anyone could turn down a trip to Atlantic City.

THE WIFE. Let's gettyup. Get the bag.

THE HUSBAND. I can't carry them any further. My back hurts. *He puts his hand to his back.* It hurts right here. . . . *Moving his hand.* And it hurts a little bit up here. . . And a little more over here. . . And it hurts real bad here whenever I try to lift luggage, especially other people's luggage . . . . And it hurts between my shoulders and in my neck and down my arms. . . . And I have this pain in my finger. . . . And here in the other finger—a hangnail. . . . And here on my chin and inside my nose— a ingrown hair. And my eyes water. . . . And I'm nervous and jumpy. . . . And I have trouble sleeping nights. . . And I have watery, iron-poor blood. . . . And I'm constipated—

THE WIFE. Well, my back—

THE HUSBAND. *Your* back. *Your* back. Don't you ever stop complaining about *your* health. . . Don't you ever think of anybody but yourself?

THE WIFE. Well, let me think. *She thinks for a few seconds.* Yes, I do. Once in a while I think of *you. Affably.* Let me tell you *what* I think of you—

THE HUSBAND. *Curt.* Never mind.

THE WIFE. Pick it up. Jeez, there's only one of them.

THE HUSBAND *strains to pick up the suitcase. He barely lifts it from the floor. He gives up the effort and lets it fall.*
    The extremely loud sound-effects thud sounds when he hits the floor.

THE HUSBAND. *Indicating* THE WIFE *'s handbag.* You want me to carry *that,*

The Arrival

too?

THE WIFE *frowns and pauses. Out of character.* Whoa! Wait a sec. You're
supposed to be portraying a person who's oblivious to my condition.

THE HUSBAND. *Out of character.* Sorry. My mistake. Just making a joke. I don't
know what I was thinking.

The Wife. Not much, I'm sure.
Indicating the suitcase. Okay, let's gettyup.

THE HUSBAND *puts on a show of just remembering something.* Gotta go! . . . Nice to
know ya! . . . Fate is calling! . . . My foot doctor is calling! . . . Mommy's
calling! . . . The wild is cabling! . . . *He bolts and runs offstage to the left.*
THE WIFE *walks swiftly offstage after him.*
There is an interval.

They come back on from the left. THE WIFE *pulls* THE HUSBAND *after her by
the arm.*

THE HUSBAND. *Panting extremely heavily, hardly able to speak.* You wouldn't . . .
have . . . caught me . . . if I hadn't . . . tripped and fallen.

THE WIFE. You didn't trip and fall.

THE HUSBAND. *Still panting extremely heavily.* I didn't? . . . What . . . happened?

THE WIFE. You ran out of breath.

THE HUSBAND. *Still panting extremely heavily.* I did *(unable to speak further he pants
for seven or eight seconds, then shouts)* not! . . . *He sits down on the corner of the
suitcase.*

The Wife. Your excursions are tedious and repetitious.
*She suddenly clutches the handbag tighter to her abdomen and groans and
grimaces.*

THE HUSBAND. *Indifferent.* You aren't grunting and groaning and making
faces about anything in particular, are you, dearie?

THE WIFE. *In distress.* I think . . .. I'm going to . . . drop it . . . throw it down
. . .

THE HUSBAND *starts violently and jumps to his feet. What! What are you talking
about! Drop it?!*

THE WIFE *nods.* Yes . . . the pains . . . .

THE HUSBAND. *Here! Now! On the sidewalk! Without a doctor! In front of all these
people! In plain sight! WITHOUT A PERMIT!*

THE WIFE. Yes . . . I feel . . . the pains . . . coming . . . coming . . .

33

The Arrival

THE HUSBAND. *Wait! Wait! You can't do that here! IT'S EMBARRASSING!*

THE WIFE. The pains . . . hurt . . . the pains . . . help me . . . inside . . . quick!

THE HUSBAND. *Yes! I will! Inside! Let's go! He hastily takes her arm and draws her toward the right. He takes two or three steps. He abruptly halts. He assumes a thoughtful expression. Calmly, to himself.* Wait a minute. What am I doing? Let me think. . . . What if . . . what if we didn't go in? . . . Yes. *Matter-of-fact, to* THE WIFE. Just go ahead and drop it right here. You see, I figure it this way: if you drop it here, it'll save the price of a room and the doctor's fee, too. Yes, you just go right ahead and drop your object. *He takes her by the arm and draws her forward two or three feet. Pointing at the stage floor in front of her.* Anywhere right her.

THE WIFE. Pains . . . hurt . . . terrible . . . very soon . . . drop it . . .

THE HUSBAND. *Looking at his watch.* We haven't got all day. Take your time but hurry up.

THE WIFE *heaves a great sigh of relief. Composed.* It's all right. I was mistaken. It was just indigestion.

THE HUSBAND. *Annoyed.* What? You mean you weren't about to drop it at all?

THE WIFE. *Cheerful.* No. At least not right now. It was heartburn.

THE HUSBAND. What! Heartburn! . . . Dammit, that means I pay after all. *With abrupt exaggerated anger. Heartburn!* You have heartburn! You should have taken something for heartburn!

THE WIFE. You forget: you didn't buy me anything to take for heartburn when I asked you to buy me something for heartburn.

THE HUSBAND. *Angry.* Why not!

THE WIFE. You said you forgot, remember.

THE HUSBAND *frowns, puts his hand to his chin and considers. Calmly.* What was it you wanted.

THE WIFE. Tums Candy Mints.

THE HUSBAND. Oh well. That explains it. Tums Candy Mints are *expensive.* *He glances around. He bolts and dashes offstage to the left.*
THE WIFE *walks rapidly off after him.*
There is a loud crashing sound offstage on the left.
There is an interval.

34

The Arrival

THE WIFE *and* THE HUSBAND *come back on stage from the left.*
THE WIFE *leads* THE HUSBAND *by the ear.* THE HUSBAND *limps. He holds his hand to his head and grimaces in pain.*
THE HUSBAND. What happened? I was running down the road . . .
THE WIFE. You ran off the road and ran into a tree.
THE HUSBAND. I did? How did that happen?
THE WIFE. You were running too fast for road conditions.
    THE HUSBAND *sits down on the suitcase.*
THE WIFE. Come on. Let's go.
THE HUSBAND. *Placid.* Oh what's the rush? . . . I'd really rather not. Why don't we just sit here for a little while? I kind of like it here. The climate's agreeable.
THE WIFE. Come on.
THE HUSBAND. *Feigning distraction.* Look. What a beautiful view. . . . and look at the sky—it's so—how can I describe it?—*blue.*
THE WIFE. All right. I'll go on by myself.
THE HUSBAND. Go ahead. Won't do you any good. Of course they won't give you a room. You don't have any money with you.
THE WIFE. I don't need any money. I'll charge everything to you.
THE HUSBAND *frowns. Uncertain.* You can't do that. *Definite.* You can't do that.
THE WIFE. We'll see. *She begins to walk slowly to the right. Shrewd.* I'm tired. . . .
    Of course I'll get a room with a memory foam bed . . . a sauna . . .
THE HUSBAND *jumps to his feet.* Now wait! You mean you intend to go there and try to charge a luxury-priced room to me without me there to stop you?
THE WIFE *halts and faces him. Flatly.* Why yes. *She begins to walk to the right. Provoking him.* I'll have them install an eight-foot QLED TV set and a IMAX movie projector and a thirteen-foot Jacuzzi and twenty-four dozen orchids—
THE HUSBAND. *Wait! Resigned.* All right. All right. I'm coming. *Deliberating, to himself.* She *might* be bluffing but money is not something you can gamble with.
    He grips the handle of the suitcase with both hands and drags the suitcase a short distance. He lets go of the suitcase. He stands straight with a hand at his back as if from the strain.

Out of character. To The Wife. I think I've got the idea of this play. It's like this: for an unknown reason you want to go to the hospital. So here we are on the way to the hospital. But, you see, what happens is: we never get there. . . . We go to the hospital but we never get to the hospital. That's a very profound idea. I like that idea. It's brilliant.

THE WIFE. *Out of character.* Where does the fact that we *do* get to the hospital fit in?

THE HUSBAND. *Out of character.* That's the wrinkle that makes it *especially* brilliant. *He grasps the handle of the suitcase again but releases it when he sees* THE ATTENDANT (AS PORTER).

THE ATTENDANT (AS PORTER), in the Pullman porter's jacket and cap, walks on stage from the right, downstage from the counter.

THE HUSBAND. *To* THE ATTENDANT (AS PORTER). *Startled.* What the hell! What's going on here? What are *you* doing here? I thought we got rid of you. What happened to the rich guy you were talking about? It didn't take you long to cheat some money out of him, I guess.

THE HUSBAND *and* THE WIFE *sit down on corners of the suitcase.*

THE ATTENDANT (AS PORTER). It didn't work out. I have to admit—and you know me well enough to know that it is *very* seldom that I admit to *anything*—that the story is a bit of a downer. It turned out he had been hemorrhaging for six months. By that I mean his wallet had been hemorrhaging for six months. We declared him destitute and admitted him to the charity ward. When we asked him to enroll in a Time Payment Plan for Services Rendered Gratis, he said he would rather die that sign. . . . And he was true to his word.

THE HUSBAND. So what happened to his luggage?

THE ATTENDANT (AS PORTER). I stole it.

THE HUSBAND. That makes you a thief.

THE ATTENDANT (AS PORTER). One of many things of which I am composed, I assure you.

A couple items.

Since your last visit, our recovery room has installed special calmative lighting. This, of course, for the purpose of imbuing a positive and optimistic mental attitude—always a good thing. This consists of 68,025 twinkling recessed ceiling bulblets. This splendid nighttime-starry-sky-like array has given us the opportunity to name a bulblet after each and every one of our customers. We have chosen the bulblets that will bear the names of you two. *He pauses briefly.* This is absolutely free and it comes with a guarantee. If your bulblet burns out within two years, it will be replaced at absolutely no cost to you. *Speaking more softly and more rapidly.* Refer to the agreement for after two years. *He pauses briefly.* No need to thank us.

THE HUSBAND. Where are our bulblets in this room?

THE ATTENDANT (AS PORTER). Very easy to locate. Directly above the "t" in the Restrooms sign.

Let me continue, please.

Mr. . . . *(he clears his throat),* our great enterprise takes great pleasure in recognizing the loyalty of our great customers. Not only. We take equal, or, indeed, greater, pleasure in rewarding that loyalty. I am, personally, pleased to award you with our loyalty card. It conveys to you exclusive membership in our rewards program. In addition to countless other benefits, it entitles you to an up-front discount of ought point ought one seven seven six percent on any of our services without restriction. *Speaking more softly and rapidly.* Terms and conditions may apply.

Handing THE HUSBAND *a card.* Congratulations! You are now an official member of what we have named our Charmed Circle . . . in full the Charmed Circle of Jerks. Enjoy.

THE HUSBAND. Oh, thanks.

THE ATTENDANT (AS PORTER). Glad to do it. It's nothing . . .

If you'll just bear with me for one more, last thing. *Handing* THE HUSBAND *a business card.* Let me give you another card—my business card. I have a business on the side. It's a catering service. I've named it Engorge Incorporated. Kind of catchy, huh? If you need catering service or perhaps a friend or even an enemy, please keep me in mind. There are specialty functions in which we particularly excel. These include drunken wakes, divorce celebrations, and circumcision celebrations.

Now before I go just let me quickly complete my task by removing your carcasses from the luggage and I'll do that and be on my way.

THE WIFE *and* THE HUSBAND *get up from the suitcase.* THE ATTENDANT

(AS PORTER) *steps to the suitcase, picks it up easily, swiftly carries it to the right, and sets it down three feet or so in front of the counter.*

There you are, sir. And I'm on my way. *Au revoir. Singing à the song,* We'll meet again. *Speaking.* We don't know when but we do know where, right? *He walks offstage to the right, downstage from the counter.*

THE HUSBAND *and* THE WIFE *sit back down on corners of the suitcase, more or less facing the audience.*

THE HUSBAND. *To* THE WIFE. I don't know. Maybe that jerk wasn't so bad. He didn't get any money out of me.

THE ATTENDANT (AS PORTER). *Shouting from offstage from the right.* WHILE YOU WEREN'T LOOKING, I STOLE YOUR BALANCE DUE FROM YOU!

THE HUSBAND. *To* THE WIFE. Did you hear that?

THE WIFE. Yes

THE HUSBAND. I didn't.

#

THE WIFE *and* THE HUSBAND, *whose backs are to the clothes tree, do not observe any of the following.*

THE ATTENDANT (AS PORTER) *steps on stage from the right, upstage from the counter. He walks to the clothes tree. He takes off his porter's jacket and hangs it on the clothes tree. He takes a hotel front desk clerk's jacket from the clothes tree and puts it on. He takes off his porter's cap and hangs it on the clothes tree. He takes a front desk clerk's receptionist's cap and puts it on.*

The front desk clerk's jacket is a maroon blazer with brass buttons and the front desk clerk's cap is a black-and-white baseball cap.

THE ATTENDANT (AS DESK CLERK) *walks offstage where he walked on stage.*

He walks on stage from the right, downstage from the counter, and steps behind the counter.

ringing the desk call bell

LEFT OFF

START POINT

\#

THE ATTENDANT (AS DESK CLERRK). *In an official tone.* Please excuse my

absence. It was a matter of . . . of urgency.

THE HUSBAND. *Aggressively.* Where were you?

THE ATTENDANT (AS DESK CLERRK). Why . . . I . . . as a matter of fact, I was
visiting the biffey.

THE HUSBAND. Who's she?

THE ATTENDANT (AS DESK CLERRK). I mean, sir, I was in the convenience.

THE HUSBAND. Was it inconvenient? You're damn right it was inconvenient.
We had to wait for you.

THE ATTENDANT (AS DESK CLERRK). I was in the sanitary, sir.

THE HUSBAND. "Sanitary"?

THE WIFE *walks to* THE HUSBAND, *draws his head down and whispers in his
ear.*

THE HUSBAND *abruptly stands erect and exclaims.* Bathroom!

THE WIFE *draws* THE HUSBAND's *head down again and whispers in is ear.*

THE HUSBAND *stands erect.* Now I understand. You were in the
bathroom—*(he pauses)*—where you were—*(he pauses again and looks* at
THE ATTENDANT (AS DESK CLERRK) *and* THE WIFE, *who
frowns)*—washing your hands. He *looks at them and smiles. Affably.* You didn't
have to worry about what I'd say. If there's one thing I'd never say out
loud it's that you were in the bathroom where you were *icky-pooing. He
claps his hand over his mouth.*

THE ATTENDANT (AS DESK CLERRK). Speaking as just one more armchair
psychoanalyst, sir, my guess is that there's some kind of defect in your
inhibitory mechanism.

THE HUSBAND. You mean, sometimes I blab by accident? overwhelmed by
your insignificance HELP NEEDED

THE ATTENDANT (AS DESK CLERRK). You understand my analysis perfectly, sir. Are you an enthusiast, too? . . . He clears his throat and rubs his hands together. s. Well, here you two pigeons are. You've finally arrived. It took you long enough.

THE HUSBAND. No, it didn't. It didn't take us long *enough*. We—

THE ATTENDANT (AS DESK CLERRK) *holds out his hand as a signal to be silent.* Excuse me for a moment. Paperwork, you understand. You don't have any reason to be in a hurry, do you?

THE HUSBAND *starts. Quickly.* No! Oh no. No reason at all.

THE ATTENDANT (AS DESK CLERRK) *shuffles through the papers on the stand, takes folded papers from his pockets, unfolds them, puts them with other papers, takes a paper, folds it and puts it in his pocket, takes out a notebook and pen, makes a note in the notebook, makes notes on papers, takes a pile of papers from the stand, rearranges them, searches through another pile of papers. shuffles through a pile of file cards and searches through the pages of a ledge.*

He takes a paper, crumples it and tosses it to the floor, searches through some papers, takes another paper, crumples it and tosses it to the floor. He begins to shuffle through some papers and suddenly stops. He pauses. He walks quickly to the second paper he has thrown to the floor, picks it up, uncrumples it, takes it to the stand, smooths it out and puts it among other paper. He pauses again, turns and look at the first paper he has thrown to the floor. He walks to it slowly, his hand at his chin as if he is thinking. He halts near the paper. He shakes his head and begins to walk back towards the stand. Suddenly he turns around and walks quickly to the paper, kicks it violently away and walk quickly back to the stand. He leans over the stand.

THE HUSBAND. Our—

THE ATTENDANT (AS DESK CLERRK). Excuse me, sir. As you can see, I am a busy, busy, busy man. And no wonder: business is thriving. We're very, very, very busy. Business is busyness. B.U.S.Y. You understand, sir? I made up that motto myself. I'm very gifted. The crush of customers is almost unbelievable.

THE HUSBAND. *Looking around.* It looks to me like we're the only people here.

THE ATTENDANT (AS DESK CLERK). Looks around. My goodness, you're right. I really hadn't noticed. *He puzzles.* I wonder . . . *After three or four seconds the thought suddenly occurs to him.* Oh! No doubt we're on lockdown

and everyone is sheltering in place. This is an open carry state. We—by
that I mean the company—have had our incidents. Have we ever! But let
us not allow ourselves to be distracted by spectacle when our
concentration should be on our sole service goal—

THE HUSBAND. *Interrupting.* Making money.

THE ATTENDANT (AS DESK CLERK). *Quickly, flatly.* Far from it: making *you*
happy.

In conformance with which it would please *me* ever so much to be able
to tell you something other than what I am about to tell you. The fact of the
matter—and we are sometimes disappointed by the world's truths, are we
not?—is that if you don't have a reservation, I'm not at all sure I can squeeze
you in. You may have to take what you can get and pay for what you take.
But we'll come to that.

> *He shuffles more papers and riffles more cards, carelessly letting them fall to the
> floor.*

THE HUSBAND, *indicating the scattered papers and cards.* What are you *doing*?

THE ATTENDANT (AS DESK CLERK). I don't know what I'm looking for, but
maybe I'll find it anyway.

To THE HUSBAND. Is this for you or your pet?

THE HUSBAND. Not us. Not pet.

THE WIFE. For me.

THE ATTENDANT (AS DESK CLERK) *to* THE HUSBAND. You don't know
how lucky you are, sir. The prices in our veterinarian division are just
unbelievable.

Do you have a pet?

THE HUSBAND. No.

THE WIFE. Yes.

THE ATTENDANT (AS DESK CLERK), *addressing the both of them.* What kind of
pet is that?

THE HUSBAND. No pet.

THE WIFE. A dog.

THE ATTENDANT (AS DESK CLERK). Oh? What kind of dog?

THE HUSBAND. No pet. No dog.

THE WIFE. A Japanese terrier.

THE ATTENDANT (AS DESK CLERK). Japanese, huh?

THE HUSBAND. No pet. No dog. No Japanese.

THE ATTENDANT (AS DESK CLERK). Male or female.

THE HUSBAND. No male. No female.

THE WIFE. Male.

THE ATTENDANT (AS DESK CLERK). You could bring it in.

THE HUSBAND. What for?

THE ATTENDANT (AS DESK CLERK). To get him circumcised.

THE HUSBAND *considers for a moment.* No, I—

THE ATTENDANT (AS DESK CLERK), *interrupting.* We could give you a rate . . .

THE HUSBAND. No, I don't—

THE ATTENDANT (AS DESK CLERK), *interrupting.* We could give you the foreskin as a memento . . .

THE HUSBAND. Not really . . . no . . . not at this time . . .

THE ATTENDANT (AS DESK CLERK). Some of our customers have been able to wear it on their pinky.

THE HUSBAND. *Looking at one of his hands, considering.* No . . . I don't know how big that would be. . . . I think my hand would be too big for that. . . .

THE ATTENDANT (AS DESK CLERK). O-*kay,* you can't say you didn't have your chance . . .

He stands up straight and hikes up the sleeves of his jacket and shirt. He leans over the stand on his elbows and smiles amiably.

THE ATTENDANT (AS DESK CLERK). Now, then. *He clears his throat.* Getting down to business. *Reciting a set piece.* It is my duty as well as my very great pleasure as desk clerk and worker of the week to extend to you the warmest of possible welcomes on behalf of the staff and the management, and, indeed, on behalf of the ownership, the only ones that count.

He smiles broadly and walks in front of the stand. He shakes THE WIFE's hand. Welcome to you, ma'am. He shakes THE HUSBAND's hand. Welcome to you, sir. He walks behind the desk. It certainly is wonderful to have you here at . . . *(he stammers, as if he forgets his speech)* at . . . to have you here at . . . . Oh *damn!* He takes a small pocket-size booklet from his pocket and begins to leaf through it. *He looks up at* THE HUSBAND *and* THE WIFE *and speaks matter-of-factly in response to their puzzled looks.* It's a little book that tells us what to say to the customers. It's provided by the company. Very useful.

THE HUSBAND. You mean you were just reciting that about how wonderful it is to have us here?

THE ATTENDANT (AS DESK CLERK). Yes, sir. And a very good piece of writing it is, don't you think? *He smiles and continues to leaf through the book.* Hmm. *He looks at a page. He reads:* "Please excuse my temporary absence." "Where were you?" "Why, as a matter of fact I was visiting the biffy." No, that's not what we want. He turns over two or three pages. Ah, here we are. "Welcome to you sir. It certainly is wonderful to have you here at——." Hah! No wonder I couldn't remember what the next words are! There's a coffee stain on the page! It covers them up! *He considers.* It must have happened at the snack bar. *As if he remembers.* Ah, yes, I remember. I spilled my coffee on this when a waitress slapped me for giving her the goose. *He looks at the book closely.* I can't make out what it says. . . . ". . . to have you here at . . . ." "Happy Valley Hospital"? . . . "Pleasant Meadow Hospital"? . . . "Sunny West Side Hospital?"? Oh well, I suppose one hospital is as good as another.

However, to continue. *He reads:* " 'Believe me when I say that I sincerely welcome you from the bottom of my heart. I welcome you 'with a ring for your finger, shoes for your feet and a fatted calf.' " *He stops reading and frowns.* "Rings"? "Shoes"? "Fatted calf"? What does that mean? He looks at the book more closely. Maybe there are footnotes. . . . No.

THE WIFE. It's from the Bible.

THE ATTENDANT (AS DESK CLERK). *With feigned enthusiasm.* Is it now? . . . Of course, the Bible. I've got one of those things at home. *He recites:* "To be or not to be . . . ." The Bible . . . yes, it's a very good book. . . . it makes a good kitchen-door stop.

He pauses, looking at THE WIFE *closely.* Madam, I'm catching from your expression that you are surprised and disgusted by my unreluctance to reveal my lack of knowledge. Please keep in mind that working this job I am not paid for my *knowledge. He pauses briefly.* I am paid for my *charm. He smiles a forced, exaggeratedly broad smile.*

He again reads from the book: "Believe me when I say that I sincerely—"

He breaks off. Humph. That's enough of *that. He picks up the book, slaps it closed and tosses it away.* Affably. I like to give a personal, individual welcome to the customers, aside from all this that the company makes me recite to them. *He walks in front of the counter and shakes hands with* THE WIFE. How do you do, ma'am. My name is Clark, or Clerk, as we say in America. Nice to meet you. *He shakes hands with* THE HUSBAND. How do you do sir, My name is Clark, or Clerk, as we say in America. Nice to meet you. He goes behind the counter and leans over it. I may be old-fashioned but I don't think anything can replace a personal, individual welcome.

He takes his hands from the counter, hikes up the sleeves of his jacket and shirt and places his hands back on the stand. So if you're not in an awful *rush—he breaks off as if he thinks of something—*you're not in an awful rush, are you?

THE HUSBAND. *Quickly.* No! No. Not at all. At least I know *I'm* not.

THE ATTENDANT (AS DESK CLERK). Good. I knew you'd say you weren't. *To* THE WIFE. And you, ma'am, are you in an awful rush?

THE WIFE. Yes.

THE ATTENDANT (AS DESK CLERK). So if you're not in an awful rush, then, we can chat for a few minutes and get to know a little something about each other. We'll become fast friends and do each other favors. Let's start off by gossiping, shall we? You tell me about your Aunt Bertha, who prefers Brussels sprouts to broccoli and I'll tell you about my grandfather, who was a train-robber, and about a certain man I happen to know about, Mr. Porpoupoulos, the pederast. . . . There, now, we're practically fast friends already, aren't we?

THE HUSBAND. Well . . . I guess so . . . yes . . . .

THE ATTENDANT (AS DESK CLERK). Good. Then lend me fifty dollars.

THE HUSBAND. Well . . . no . . . I . . . can't . . . .

THE ATTENDANT (AS DESK CLERK) *assumes a disappointed expression.* Are you quite sure you can't? Remember our friendship.

THE HUSBAND. Well . . . no . . . really . . . I can't . . . . THE ATTENDANT (AS DESK CLERK) gestures with his hand, dismissing the idea.

THE ATTENDANT (AS DESK CLERK). Well, sir, I guess you've got some kind of a gripe about your health. Most of the people do who come in here. At least, I can't think of any other reason they'd have anything to do with the quacks around here. So you might indicate to me now just what specifically your gripe is—not that I personally care in the least, of course.

THE HUSBAND. Well, it's my wife. She's got this idea that—

THE ATTENDANT (AS DESK CLERK). You're not going to tell me your marital troubles, are you, sir? *I* don't want to hear them. Let me recommend my *brother:* he happens to be a really first-rate marriage counselor. Here's his card. *He hands* THE HUSBAND *a business card.*

THE HUSBAND. Haltingly. My wife . . . I'm not sure exactly what's wrong with her . . . upset stomach . . . there's a little pain—so she says . . . swelling . . . colitis . . . heartburn . . . indigestion . . . spots in front of her eyes. . . . . She knits a lot . . . and eats chalk . . . it's probably just neuritis . . . stomachitis . . . maybe just mutiple endocrine neoplasia syndrome type 2. . . . She needs rest . . . relaxation . . . fresh air . . . warm milk . . . weak tea . . . .

THE ATTENDANT (AS DESK CLERK). *Enthusiastic.* You are very lucky to have come to us, sir! We have just the facilities required in such cases! Our man in this field is the best in the country!

THE HUSBAND. *Indifferently.* That so?

THE ATTENDANT (AS DESK CLERK). *Enthusiastically.* Yes! I have diagnosed the case conclusively! Your wife is about to have a *baby!*

THE HUSBAND *clutches his abdomen, screws up his face and doubles over.*

THE ATTENDANT (AS DESK CLERK). What is it, sir! What's the matter! Are you sick? THE HUSBAND *nods.* Something you ate, sir? THE HUSBAND *shakes his head.* Something I said? THE HUSBAND *nods.*

I believe you may be desperately ill, sir. Are you sure you haven't come to the wrong place? The emergency desk is three doors down.

To THE WIFE. Perhaps you know first aid, ma'am? If not I may have to call one of the doctors here and your husband will just have to take his chances.

THE HUSBAND *grimaces in pain and groans loudly.*

THE ATTENDANT (AS DESK CLERK) *slaps him in the face.* Here! Here! Shut up! Shut up, sir! Stop that! I won't have that! *To* THE WIFE, *explaining.* I hate to see a person suffer.

THE HUSBAND *stops grimacing and groaning. He stands clutching his abdomen. There is a sickly expression on his face.*

THE ATTENDANT (AS DESK CLERK). Feeling better, sir!

THE HUSBAND. *Haltingly.* Yes. I've . . . already . . . almost . . . forgotten . . . what you said.

THE ATTENDANT (AS DESK CLERK) *frowns.* That's strange. I've forgotten what I said myself. . . . Now isn't that something? . . . I'm getting to be as bad as you, sir. . . As a businessman, of course, I find it difficult to retain trivial information that doesn't affect my vital interests. . . . *He thinks.* What was it I said? . . . Was it—? THE HUSBAND clutches his abdomen with one hand. He holds up the other and shakes his head. as a signal to be silent.

THE ATTENDANT (AS BELLHOP) *gives up trying to remember.* Oh well. I'm sure it wasn't important. . . . My advice to you, sir, is that you should definitely be more particular about your hearing habits.

He fumbles among the papers. Some of them fall to the floor. He takes up some file cards from the stand. He riffles through them carelessly, dropping several of them. He selects one of them and takes a pen from his pocket. He puts the pen on the counter. He hikes up his sleeves and clears his throat. He takes up the pen again. I'm going to ask you some personal questions now so that I can fill out this little file card here, thereby continuing to put on the appearance of efficiency—an appearance which—I'm sure you will agree—I have so far sustained remarkably well. . . . What is your name, sir?

THE HUSBAND *opens his mouth as if he is about to speak and closes it as if he forgets what he intends to say. Speaking as if out of character to the audience.* Now is when I'm supposed to go and forget what my name is supposed to be. Which is pretty stupid because it just ain't realistic: it's the simplest name there is: Jones. So I'll just skip over that part of the play. *Indicating* THE DIRECTOR. *I guess this guy is trying to be funny writing it so I forget something nobody could ever forget in a million years. To* THE ATTENDANT (AS DESK CLERK). My name is Jones.

THE WIFE *quickly corrects him. She prompts him in a loud whisper.* Smith.

THE HUSBAND. *Quickly correcting himself in a loud voice, slapping his hands to his forehead.* Smith! *He makes embarrassed gestures.* My name is Smith!

THE ATTENDANT (AS DESK CLERK). *Writing on the card.* Smith. . . . That's a common name. *He looks at* THE HUSBAND *from head to foot.* Common man. *He pauses.* First name.

THE HUSBAND. *As if what he says is obvious.* John.

THE ATTENDANT (AS DESK CLERK). Middle initial?

THE HUSBAND. Quincy.

THE ATTENDANT (AS DESK CLERK) *looks up at him and frowns.* I said your middle *initial.* sir. *He holds out the card and points to it.* See there. It says middle initial. I can't possibly write a full name in that little box. Now then—what is your middle initial.

THE HUSBAND. Quentin.

THE ATTENDANT (AS DESK CLERK). *Nearing the end of his patience.* Please, sir! Just tell me what your middle initial is!

THE HUSBAND. *As if relenting.* Q.

THE ATTENDANT (AS DESK CLERK). *Relieved.* Ah. Thank you. *Writing.* Q. *Gravely.* I suggest you be more cooperative as we move along, sir. You've wasted precious seconds of my time. I belong to fourteen business and professional associations so you can imagine how valuable my time is. I'm sticking you thirty-five dollars and thirty-eight cents as fitting compensation to me for your display of recalcitrance. *He writes on a paper.* . . . *Reflectively* . Q. That's an unusual middle initial you've got there. What does it stand for? . . . Quentin? . . . Quincy?

THE HUSBAND. Quogg.

THE ATTENDANT (AS DESK CLERK). Oh? You don't say?

THE HUSBAND. Yes. I was named for my grandmother back in England.

THE ATTENDANT (AS DESK CLERK). Oh? What was her name?

THE HUSBAND. Quirt.

THE ATTENDANT (AS DESK CLERK). Is that a fact? You know, incidentally, I knew a kid once in elementary school called Quirt. I remember his name was Samuel. Sam Quirt. We called his Squirt for short. And you know what? He *was* a squirt . . . a nothing . . . a zero . . . *Reflectively.* Why, I haven't thought about Squirt for ages. . . . Ah, sweet, sweet memory! . . . It's so pleasant to remember things, isn't it, sir?

THE HUSBAND. I prefer to forget them, myself.

THE ATTENDANT (AS DESK CLERK) *clears his throat. In a businesslike tone, indicating* THE WIFE. And this, sir, is your wife, let us hope, rather than a very good—not to say intimate—girl friend?

THE HUSBAND. Yes.

THE ATTENDANT (AS DESK CLERK). Good. Marriage is so much the superior course.

THE HUSBAND. Is that right? Why do say that?

THE ATTENDANT (AS DESK CLERK). My other brother is in the wedding business. *Writing on the card.* Wife's name: Jane.

THE HUSBAND. Hey, wait a minute. How do you know my wife's name is Jane?

THE ATTENDANT (AS DESK CLERK). Your name is Smith, isn't it? Your name is John, isn't it? This is your wife, isn't it? So what else *could* your wife's name be?

THE HUSBAND. Mary.

THE ATTENDANT (AS DESK CLERK). But it's not.

THE HUSBAND. No, it's Jane.

THE ATTENDANT (AS DESK CLERK) *writes on the file card and tosses it to the floor.*

THE ATTENDANT (AS DESK CLERK). Of course your wife made you make a reservation in order to insure that it would be impossible for you to claim that you couldn't get a room because all the rooms were taken, thereby saving yourself money.

THE HUSBAND nods.

THE ATTENDANT (AS DESK CLERK). Now let me pretend to look for a record of your reservation. Because of course it just so happens that if I can't find a record of your reservation, the only rooms we have available are among our more . . .our more outrageously priced accommodations. *He shuffles some papers. He searches through papers and registers. He takes up a book and looks at the inscription on its spine, puts it down and searches further. He takes up another book, turns over some pages and smooths them. He runs his finger down the page. He starts.* Ah!

THE HUSBAND. You found it?

THE ATTENDANT (AS DESK CLERK) *holds up the book. He turns it upside down. He puts it down and searches in it. He bends over the book and looks at it closely.* My writing's a little hard to read: I write a perfect round hand. *He scrutinizes the page. He roughly turns a page, tearing a large corner of the page away in his hand. He scrutinizes both sides of the corner. He tosses it to the floor.* Do you have a confirm?

That Husband. What's that?

THE WIFE. A confirmation, you idiot.

THE HUSBAND *frowns and glares at* THE WIFE. If you're going to start insulting me, I'm leaving. *He steps to the left.*

THE WIFE *catches the tail of his jacket and pulls him back to the counter.*

THE HUSBAND. No, I don't have a confirmation. That settles it. We can't stay here. We have to go. *To* THE WIFE. Let's go. He again steps to the left. THE WIFE *again catches the tail of his jacket and pulls him back.*

THE ATTENDANT (AS DESK CLERK). Oh no, oh no. You can't get away that easy, sir. . . . *He tears out the page of the register. He crumples it into a ball and throws it to the floor. Explaining.* You were smudged.

THE HUSBAND. *Inspecting his clothes.* Where?

THE ATTENDANT (AS DESK CLERK). Your name was smeared. The ink was wet. Naturally the room has been taken by another party. *In a tone of exaggerated disappointment.* And I'm so sorry: we're absolutely filled to capacity.

THE WIFE. *To* THE HUSBAND. Aren't you going to say something facetious about there not being room at the inn.

THE HUSBAND. Inn? What inn?

THE ATTENDANT (AS DESK CLERK). In point of fact, there is always room at the inn, which, as you may know, is in this country called the cafeteria. I would not recommend attendance at that place. We could install a cot in the hallway leading to the emergency exit.

THE HUSBAND. *Very eager. Exit?! Did you say "exit"?! I'll take it!*

THE ATTENDANT (AS DESK CLERK). Upon further reflection, something of minimally acceptable desirability may possibly be possible. . . .

THE HUSBAND. *Damn. . . .* We can't stay here. I don't have any money. Nice talking to you. Good-by. *To* THE WIFE. Let's go. *He takes a step to the left.* THE WIFE *again catches the tail of his jacket and pulls him back.*

THE ATTENDANT (AS DESK CLERK). I have absolutely no fear about getting our money out of you, sir. *His tone suddenly becomes menacing.* Because we *always* get our money out of our customers.

THE HUSBAND. *Aggressively.* Not this time.

THE ATTENDANT (AS DESK CLERK). *Flatly, without menace.* Every time, sir.

THE HUSBAND. *Angrily.* I'll refuse to pay!

THE ATTENDANT (AS DESK CLERK). *Flatly.* We'll extort it form you, sir.

THE HUSBAND. *Calmly, puzzled.* "Extort" it?

THE ATTENDANT (AS DESK CLERK). Beat it out of you, sir.

THE HUSBAND. *Shouting angrily. Just you try it!*

THE ATTENDANT (AS DESK CLERK). *Flatly.* Certainly sir, if necessary. *There is an interval.*

THE HUSBAND. Aren't you going to jabber some more? I've got plenty of time to listen, you know, not being in a rush or anything like that.

THE ATTENDANT (AS DESK CLERK). *Writing in the register.* Single for Mrs. Jones—

THE HUSBAND. *Vehemently.* Smith! My name is Smith!

THE ATTENDANT (AS DESK CLERK) *shrugs his shoulders indifferently.* All right, if you prefer: for Mrs. Smith. . . . Deluxe Princess Suite—

THE HUSBAND. I'm not taking the Princess Suite. That'll be the day I take the Princess Suite. Give her the cheapest room you've got. She only needs a room to rest and relax in for a couple of minutes. Besides it would be cheaper.

THE ATTENDANT (AS DESK CLERK). I explained that to you a few lines back, sir. The only space we have—

THE HUSBAND. We'll be going. Good-by. *To* THE WIFE. Let's go. Come on. *He takes a step to the left.* THE WIFE *again catches the tail of his coat and pulls him back.*

THE ATTENDANT (AS DESK CLERK). Wait, sir! Let me try this approach: I just now happened to find something inexpensive available that I hadn't noticed before.

THE HUSBAND. You did? *Damn. . . .* I still won't take it. It's not cheap enough.

THE ATTENDANT (AS DESK CLERK). I'll accommodate you there, sir: I'll say this: it's *dirt cheap.* How's that?

THE HUSBAND. *Hesitating.* Well . . . maybe . . . all right. *He frowns. He abruptly smiles. He puts his hands in his pockets. He thrusts out his chest and bounces on his heels. Scoffing.* Hah! You thought you'd trick me into taking a luxury-priced room, didn't you? Because you don't make so much on a cheap room, do you? Huh? Do you?

THE ATTENDANT (AS DESK CLERK). *Politely.* That's true, sir, we usually don't. But I think we might be able to make a special exception in your case, sir. We might be able to make a special provision and overcharge you more than is usual. . *He abruptly puts on a show of exaggerated embarrassment.* Please, sir! Don't thank me! Say no more, please! *In a pious tone.* I am content with the knowledge that I have been of service. "Giveth it to him that asketh." *To* THE WIFE, *flatly.* That's from the Bible, too, isn't it? *To* THE HUSBAND, *piously.* I would do the same to anyone.

So, you two, let me summarize our interaction today by saying it has been a privilege to serve you. I *feel* privileged. In fact, I *am* privileged. But nothing I haven't earned by hook or by crook.

Speaking of economics, besides also being an arm-chair rocket scientist, I am an arm-chair political scientist hyphen economist. I have distilled the political slash economic system of these great United States into just one single principle, which I might test out on you, if you will allow me, since it pertains to you.

THE HUSBAND. Me? Really?

THE ATTENDANT (AS DESK CLERK). It is this: There is no person or process that is too insignificant—okay, here we are: insignificant person equals you—or too significant—here again: significant process equals the process you are involved in—okay, let me back up and start at the beginning so it's clear: There is no person or process that is too insignificant or too significant that it does not merit attention *(after a slight pause, quickly)* for the purpose of profit. Agree? Disagree?

THE HUSBAND. Well, I don't—

THE WIFE. There's a certain amount of wisdom to that.

The Arrival

THE HUSBAND. I'm not sure . . . maybe . . . What's this "profit"? . . . Who's
doing the profiting? . . . I don't know. . . . I'll think about it. . . .
THE ATTENDANT (AS DESK CLERK). While you do that, sir, I'll call the
bellhop for you.
THE HUSBAND. *Firm.* No. Don't call a bellhop. I don't need a bellhop. *He
steps swiftly to the suitcase. He picks it up hastily and it slips out of his hands. At the
moment it hits the floor, the very loud sound effects thud sounds.*
Shouting angrily. Call a bellhop!
THE ATTENDANT (AS DESK CLERK). *Calmly.* Certainly, sir. *He shouts. Front! . . .*
Front! . . . He'll be here in a minute, sir. He'll have to tear himself away from
the book he's reading. He's a very intelligent and ambitious young man. He's
giving himself quite an education in his spare moments: he studies manuals.
Sex manuals.
THE ATTENDANT (AS DESK CLERK), THE WIFE, and THE HUSBAND stand
waiting for about twenty seconds.
THE HUSBAND. *Sarcastic.* Maybe he's in the biffy.
THE ATTENDANT (AS DESK CLERK). I'll go see if I can find him.
THE HUSBAND. Don't bother. We're leaving. *He grasps* THE WIFE *'s arm and
takes a step to the left.. She does not move and pulls him back by the tail of his jacket.
Meanwhile,* THE ATTENDANT (AS DESK CLERK), *who has paid no attention to* THE
HUSBAND, *walks to the right and walks offstage, downstage from the counter.*

#

THE WIFE *and* THE HUSBAND *sit down again on the corners of the suitcase, with
their backs to the clothes tree.*
*The Attendant (as desk clerk) walks on stage, upstage from the counter, and walks to
the clothes trees. He takes off his hotel receptionist's jacket and hangs it on the clothes tree.
He takes the bellhops jacket from the clothes tree and puts it on. He takes off his hotel
receptionist's hat and hangs it on the clothes tree. He takes the bellhop's jacket from the
clothes tree and puts it on. He hangs the hotel receptionist's hat on the clothes tree and
takes a bellhop's cap and puts it on.*
The bellhop's pillbox cap and bolero jacket are identical or similar to those worn by

Johnny Roventini in Philip Morris cigarette commercials.
    THE ATTENDANT (AS BELLHOP) *walks to the right and walks offstage where he walked on stage.*

                                    #

    THE ATTENDANT (AS BELLHOP) *walks on stage from the right, downstage from the counter.*
    The lights on the sofa come up full.
    When they see him, THE WIFE *and* THE HUSBAND *stand up.*
THE ATTENDANT (AS BELLHOP). *To* THE Wife *and* THE HUSBAND. You asked for a bellhop? Sir? Madam?.
    Simultaneously:
The Wife. Yes.
THE HUSBAND. No.
The Husband. It was a mistake. You can go now.
The Wife. In reality, we could use your help.
THE HUSBAND *glares at* THE WIFE *and shouts angrily at* THE ATTENDANT (AS BELLHOP). *Pick up that bag and carry it to the dirt cheap room! And don't hurry! Take your time!*
    THE ATTENDANT (AS BELLHOP) *picks up the suitcase. He picks it up with no noticeable difficulty.*
    THE ATTENDANT (AS BELLHOP) *and* THE WIFE *halt at the center of the stage, near the sofa.*
THE HUSBAND *continues to walk to the left.* THE WIFE *catches the tail of his jacket and pulls him back.*
THE HUSBAND. *Shouting angrily at* THE ATTENDANT (AS BELLHOP), *who stands*
        holding the suitcase. Put the bag over there, punk! *He points near the sofa.*
THE ATTENDANT (AS BELLHOP) *drops the suitcase. At the moment it hits the floor,*
        the very loud sound-effects thud sounds. THE ATTENDANT (AS BELLHOP) *violently*
        seizes the THE HUSBAND's *lapels and shakes him. Shouting.* You call me a punk,
        sir? Don't call me a punk! I'll bash your goddam head in, sir!
THE HUSBAND. *Stern.* Are you threatening me?
THE ATTENDANT (AS BELLHOP). *Shouting. I'll knock your goddam teeth down your*

                                    53

goddam throat, sir!

THE HUSBAND *grimaces. Puzzled.* That's funny. The other guy didn't act like this. This guy acts like he thinks he actually amounts to somebody. . . . Maybe he's got a slice of Berkshire Hathaway. . . .

THE ATTENDANT (AS BELLHOP). Shouting. *And don't you forget it, sir! Abruptly calm, he releases* THE HUSBAND's *lapels.* Would you like me to leave your suitcase near the sofa, sir?

THE HUSBAND. *Shouting. Please leave my suitcase near the sofa!*

THE ATTENDANT (AS BELLHOP) *picks up the suitcase and sets it down near the sofa.*

THE WIFE. *To* THE ATTENDANT (AS BELLHOP). *Provoking, ironic.* It seems to me you have been discourteous to my husband. Should I ask him if he will let that pass?

THE HUSBAND. I refuse to answer any such question.

THE ATTENDANT (AS BELLHOP) *walks to* THE HUSBAND *and holds out his hand for his tip.*

THE HUSBAND. That's fine. You can go now. THE ATTENDANT (AS BELLHOP) *is silent. He continues to hold out his hand.* That's it. Very good. You can go now. You've done a real fine job. Thank you very much. We'll call you if we need you again. Do you have a business card? We'll be in touch. THE ATTENDANT (AS BELLHOP) *continues to hold out his hand.* Don't you want to go someplace else? I know *I'd* like to go someplace else. *He starts as if he thinks of something.* That's it. You stay here and I'll go. *He makes to walk to the left.* THE ATTENDANT (AS BELLHOP) *restrains him.*

THE HUSBAND *clears his throat, cross his arms on his chest, looks at his feet, coughs into his fist and looks around.* I think I heard the reception guy call you. You better get there quick. *He looks at* THE ATTENDANT (AS BELLHOP)'s *extended hand. He clears his throat and pauses. Firm.* You don't want a tip.

THE ATTENDANT (AS BELLHOP). Yes I do, sir.

THE HUSBAND. *Gruff, assured.* Was that hard work?

THE ATTENDANT (AS BELLHOP). No, sir.

THE HUSBAND. Easy, huh?

THE ATTENDANT (AS BELLHOP). Yes, sir.

THE HUSBAND. A pipe, right?

THE ATTENDANT (AS BELLHOP). Yes, sir.

THE HUSBAND *rocks on his heels. Assured,.* You don't deserve much, you know.

THE ATTENDANT (AS BELLHOP). I think different, sir.

THE HUSBAND. *Pays no attention to him.* And you're not going to get much.

THE ATTENDANT (AS BELLHOP). We'll see about that, sir.

THE HUSBAND *again pays no attention to him.* And don't think you are. *Haughty.*
Even though, as a matter of fact, I could give you lots. He takes a
handful of coins from his pocket. *He searches through them with his finger and
finally picks one out.* There you are, sonny boy: one of these and one of
those—and, hey, one of those too. *He puts the coins in* THE ATTENDANT
(AS BELLHOP)'s *hand. He smiles at him.*

THE ATTENDANT (AS BELLHOP) *frowns and looks closely at the coins.*

THE HUSBAND. You can go ahead and say thank you if you want.

THE ATTENDANT (AS BELLHOP) is silent. He quickly slips the coins into his
pocket and again holds his hand out.

THE HUSBAND. *For several seconds he looks off into the distance and hums a tune. He
looks at* THE ATTENDANT (AS BELLHOP). Are you still here?

THE ATTENDANT (AS BELLHOP). Yes, sir.

THE HUSBAND. You don't want anything, do you?

THE ATTENDANT (AS BELLHOP). Yes, sir.

THE WIFE. *Provoking. Sarcastic.* Maybe it has something to do with the size of
the tip.

THE HUSBAND *glares at* THE WIFE. I *gave* him a tip. *To* THE ATTENDANT (AS
BELLHOP). Do you—

THE ATTENDANT (AS BELLHOP). Yes, sir

THE HUSBAND. —want me to give you *more* mon—

THE ATTENDANT (AS BELLHOP). *Interrupting.* Yes, sir. I do, sir. Yes, sir.

THE HUSBAND. *Deliberate.* Well . . . another something would certainly hurt
but maybe it wouldn't kill me. *He takes out a handful of coins from his pocket
and stirs them with his finger.* Now let me see what we have here . . .

THE WIFE. *Provoking. Sarcastic.* Have any Susan B. Anthony dollar coins?

THE HUSBAND *turns and glares at* THE WIFE. *While he speaks to* THE WIFE, *he
absently keeps his hand held out in front of him. Abruptly outraged.* What! What's

the matter with you! Are you crazy! What are you talking about! Do you think I can afford to throw money away! What do you think, that I'm made of money! Do you think I'm rich! Who do you think I am, Uncle Scrooge?

While THE HUSBAND's *head is averted and he is distracted,* THE ATTENDANT (AS BELLHOP) *quickly takes all the coins from* THE HUSBAND's *hand. He takes one of the coins and puts it back. He puts the others in his pocket. He holds his hand out again.*

THE HUSBAND, *turns his head and looks at his hand.* Ah. Here we are; here's one. *He takes the coin from his hand and puts it in* THE ATTENDANT (AS BELLHOP)*'s hand.* There you are, fellow, another one.

THE ATTENDANT (AS BELLHOP) *quickly puts the coin in his pocket.* Thank you, sir? Thank you very much, sir! You are very kind, sir! I am very grateful, sir!

THE HUSBAND. *Impressed with* The Attendant (as bellhop)'s servility. That's the way to talk, my friend. That will be all. *To* The WIFE. He's not such a bad guy.

THE ATTENDANT (AS BELLHOP) *again holds out his hand.*

THE HUSBAND. Hey, now! Now just wait a minute! This is just *too much*—

THE ATTENDANT (AS BELLHOP). No sir, not enough.

THE HUSBAND and THE ATTENDANT (AS BELLHOP) glare at each other.

THE HUSBAND *thrusts his hands into his trouser pockets searching for coins. Confused. To himself.* Jeez . . . I don't what's going on here. . . . *To* THE ATTENDANT (AS BELLHOP). No coins. No more, sorry. . . . That's it. You'll have to be satisfied . . . *To himself.* . . . I thought . . . didn't I have lots of coins? . . . *Looking around at his feet, as if he might have dropped them.* What happened to them? . . .

THE WIFE. *Out of character. Addressing the audience.* Is there anyone here who doesn't know the answer to that question?

THE HUSBAND. To THE ATTENDANT (AS BELLHOP). Okay. That's it. No more. See ya later. Sorry.

THE ATTENDANT (AS BELLHOP). Paper, sir.

THE HUSBAND. Paper? You want a *check?*

THE ATTENDANT (AS BELLHOP). Paper money. Bills.

The Arrival

THE HUSBAND. Now wait a minute . . . I don't know what you're expecting
. . . you're not . . . *(as if suddenly understanding)* oh, I see, you'll give me
change. . . . sure . . . yeah, that makes sense. *He takes his wallet from an inside
pocket of his jacket. He holds a bill out to* THE ATTENDANT (AS BELLHOP).

THE ATTENDANT (AS BELLHOP) *snatches the bill from* THE HUSBAND*'s hand and
very quickly thrusts it into a pocket of his trousers. Firm.* I don't have any
change, either.

THE HUSBAND *pauses for a few second, considering.* I guess there's no choice . . . .

THE ATTENDANT (AS BELLHOP). Choice, sir?

THE HUSBAND. When nobody has any change, I guess the only thing you
can do is say "Keep the change."

THE ATTENDANT (AS BELLHOP). I concur.

The Husband *pauses for a few seconds, considering.* Keep the change.

The Attendant (as bellhop). *Abruptly wildly effusive.* Oh thank you, thank you,
sir. I am so, so grateful. Here *(he hugs The Husband).* I love you, man.
*(*THE HUSBAND *responds minimally to the hug, involuntarily putting a hand on*
THE ATTENDANT (AS BELLHOP)*'s hip.)* I'm going to remember this
moment for the rest of my life.

  You know, somehow I think you must have known of the terrible
burden I bear from my brother, who was born with—using the technical
medical term—a big head—

THE HUSBAND. *Interrupting.* Hydrocephalus. Oh, my. Tragic. Your family—

THE ATTENDANT (AS BELLHOP). *Interrupting.* Not hydrocephalus. Narcissism.
He is the most selfish person in the world, making unbelieveable
financial demands of me, the bastard. It is this burden which you
have—although in infinitesimal degree—helped lighten. For which—as I
previously expressed—I am profoundly and eternally grateful.

The Husband. Well, that's great. Glad to do it.

The Attendant (as bellhop). I will go now. *He walks to the right edge of the stage.
He halts and turns to face* THE HUSBAND. *He raises his hand in farewell.* Truly,
fair thee well, sir.

THE HUSBAND *raises his hand in response.* Well, thank you. Nice to meet you.
Have a good day. THE ATTENDANT (AS BELLHOP) *steps off stage.*

HUSBAND. *To* THE WIFE. He seemed really friendly there at the last. . . . I guess you just have to know how to handle people. . . .

He stands still for an interval, as if contemplating. Distressed and anxious, he paces the floor, with his hand intermittantly at his jaw, as if he were trying to figure out the solution to a puzzle.

Suddenly he starts, as if the reality of what has just occurred strikes him for the first time.

He clutches his breast over where his wallet is. He pats the trousers pocket where his coins had been. Ah! Money! Lettuce! Chips! Gone! Thief! I know what you've done, you sneak! You friggin' fraud! That bum! He stole my bean! I'll ring his neck until it squeaks! I'll kick him where it hurts! I'll smack him into six states! Get out of here! Get out! Get out!

THE WIFE. *Sarcastic.* Gee, give that poor really friendly guy a break, will ya?

There is an interval.

Speaking slowly, to allow her listeners to follow her thought. You know, if these things didn't happen every day, I might be motivated to remark that it seems like things are repeating themselves.

The Wife and THE HUSBAND sit on the sofa.

There is an interval.

THE HUSBAND, *looking at his watch.* What's the story? Are we at a place where there are supposed to be doctors?

#

THE ATTENDANT (AS BELLHOP) *comes on stage from the right, upstage from the counter.*

He walks to the clothes tree. He takes off the bellhop's jacket and hangs it on the clothes tree. He takes a doctor's white jacket from the coat tree and puts it on. He takes off the bellhop's cap and hangs it on the coat tree. He takes a head mirror from the clothes tree and puts it on. He takes a stethoscope from the clothes tree and hangs it around his neck. He adjusts the head mirror, the jacket and the stethoscope. He takes the doctor's bag from the clothes tree. He walks to the right and walks offstage where he walked on stage.

#

The Arrival

THE ATTENDANT (AS DOCTOR) *walks on stage from the left. He walks to the left to the sofa. He holds out his hand to* THE HUSBAND. Haven't I seen you? Aren't you what we in the trade call a troublemaker?

THE HUSBAND *shakes his hand. Flatly.* We've never met. I don't have any other children, either.

THE ATTENDANT (AS DOCTOR). *Shaking* THE WIFE's *hand.* And Mrs. Smith. How are— *He breaks off and stares at* THE WIFE's *handbag.* Oh my goodness! Oh I say! I see the problem right now. Why, you're all blown up in front like a balloon, ma'am. *Grinning mischievously.* Ah. I know what it is. *He chuckles.* You've been diddly-booing in bed. *To* THE HUSBAND. Oh you dog! Oh you devil! *He guffaws loudly.*

THE HUSBAND. Hey. You're a doctor. Doctors aren't supposed to talk like that.

THE ATTENDANT (AS DOCTOR) *quickly stands at attention and assumes an exaggeratedly serious expression. Gravely.* Of course. You're right. Forgive me. I forgot myself. *Solemnly.* One must never speak lightly of the sacred subjects of pregnancy and copulation. Biologists tell us they are among the most exalted functions of Nature—ridiculous as they certainly are. To joke about them displays a serious lack of solemnity.

THE HUSBAND. That's better.

THE ATTENDANT (AS DOCTOR). *Casually.* I'm glad you like it, sir.

That being said, let us regard the process of human reproduction in its essence. What is its essence? It is one living creature living *inside* another living creature. *Disgusted. Exclaiming. MY GOD!* Oh! Isn't that just *SO, SO GROSS!* . . . *Flatly.* Still, despite which, it's a very tidy profit-producer. . . . *To* THE WIFE. How are you ma'am? I see you've hardly changed since the last time you were here. In fact, you look exactly the same, except that you look considerably older.

THE WIFE. Thank you very much. You look exactly as crafty as you did before, yourself.

THE ATTENDANT (AS DOCTOR). Yes, but my fees have gone up. . . . Do my eyes deceive me or do you look like you might be a little tired, ma'am.

THE WIFE. It's nice to know *somebody* sees straight: I *am* tired.

THE ATTENDANT (AS DOCTOR)

You can lie down here. Take off your clothes first, please.

THE ATTENDANT (AS DOCTOR) *walks downstage. He addresses the audience as if out of character. As he speaks* THE DIRECTOR *raps the umpire's chair with the baton. He frowns and puts his finger to his lips as a signal to stop talking.* I'm sorry, folks. She isn't really going to take off her clothes now. That would involve . . . certain . . . difficulties. She'll just take off her coat. Please—

THE WIFE *interrupts him. She speaks to the audience as if out of character.* I really don't see why—

THE ATTENDANT (AS DOCTOR). *To* THE WIFE. Quiet. I'm talking. *To the audience.* Please take the coat as representing—

THE WIFE. I don't really see why he [*she indicates* THE DIRECTOR] insists on acting as if the actors weren't supposed to say these speeches that they say out of character. It's obvious to everybody that he wrote these speeches as well as the rest of the play.

THE ATTENDANT (AS DOCTOR). *Vexed.* To THE WIFE. Will you be quiet? It's not obvious to *me*. *To the audience.* As I was saying, please take the coat as representing all of her clothes. I'm sure you understand. Thank you.

    He pauses.

    I may mention that if you come to tomorrow's performance you may see her take her clothes off. It varies performance to performance.

THE WIFE. *To the audience.* Let me inject a note of truth— reality. I don't take my clothes off in any performance of this play.

    THE ATTENDANT (AS DOCTOR) *looks at her. He wears an exasperated expression. He walks back upstage. He helps her out of her coat. He holds the coat out to* THE HUSBAND. Here, sir. Hang it up. To hang up his wife's coat is a gentleman's duty. As for you, hang it up because I'm much too lazy to.

    THE HUSBAND *takes the coat and lays it across the back of the sofa. He sits on the sofa..* THE WIFE *sits in the recliner.* THE ATTENDANT (AS DOCTOR) *goes behind the chair and takes hold of the back of the recliner.*

THE ATTENDANT (AS DOCTOR). This reclines. I'll put it down for you. *He tries to manipulates the back of the chair. He is unable to get it to recline.* Umph. I don't seem to be able to get this thing to recline. . . . Wait. . . . No. That's not it. . . . *He smiles apologetically.* These things are tricky. Besides, even for a fully-licensed surgeon, I'm extraordinarily clumsy.

THE WIFE. I hope at least you don't have a license to *drive*.

THE ATTENDANT (AS DOCTOR). *Me* drive, ma'am? Oh no, no, I couldn't. Not a man of *my* condition. Of course my chauffeur drives me wherever I want to go in any one of my three television-equipped limousines.

THE WIFE. *Sarcastically.* I suppose that's the reason you became a surgeon—because you're so clumsy.

THE ATTENDANT (AS DOCTOR). *Seriously. Raising a finger.* There *is* possibly one other reason that I'm sure you can guess from what I've just said. *Earnestly.* But yes, it is one of the reasons, ma'am. Even as a child I was as clumsy as a girl. I could do everything wrong with my hands that a girl can do wrong. Even now I practice surgery by sewing—and botching the job. I also practice by ruining the insides of watches and dropping china—cheap watches and cheap china, needless to say. *The back of the recliner suddenly reclines and the foot support swings up.* Oh! There we are.

THE WIFE. That's fine. Thank you.

THE ATTENDANT (AS DOCTOR). What did I do? I didn't even know what I was doing. You see: I have abilities I don't even know I have. No wonder my fees are so high.

THE ATTENDANT (AS DOCTOR) *sits on the lounge.*

THE ATTENDANT (AS DOCTOR). *Affable. To* THE HUSBAND. Well, Mr. Smith, I suppose all this is pretty much old hat to you by this time.

THE HUSBAND. I don't know what you're talking about.

THE ATTENDANT (AS DOCTOR). *In the same tone.* You certainly are taking it calmly. You look as cool as a cucumber, as we say in the trade. As well you should, sir. There's certainly no use getting yourself all worked up about something as trivial as the birth of a *baby*.

THE HUSBAND *abruptly clutches his abdomen. He doubles over and contorts his face.*

THE ATTENDANT (AS DOCTOR). *As if he does not notice* THE HUSBAND's *actions.* But perhaps you *are* a little anxious (as is only to be expected in such cowardly cases as yourself) but perhaps you just don't give any outward indication of your anxiety. So let me assure you that everything that *can* be done *will* be done—and that you'll be *billed* for everything that *is* done—and without question some things that *aren't* done. I'll dun you for the bill myself, in fact.

THE HUSBAND *sits back in the sofa, composes his face, and takes his hands from his abdomen.*

THE ATTENDANT (AS DOCTOR). Perhaps I could be of service to you in some way while you're waiting for your wife. *He takes* THE HUSBAND's *wrist and feels his pulse.* Tell me this: are you sick?

THE HUSBAND. No.

THE ATTENDANT (AS DOCTOR). Have you been sick recently?

THE HUSBAND. No.

THE ATTENDANT (AS DOCTOR). How's your appetite?

THE HUSBAND. All right.

THE ATTENDANT (AS DOCTOR). Have you had your blood tested lately.

THE HUSBAND. I don't need my blood tested.

THE ATTENDANT (AS DOCTOR). *Mischievously, nudging him.* Don't speak too quickly, sir. It's a very good idea to have your blood tested if you've been—you know—out and about. *He grins shyly and chuckles.*

THE HUSBAND. I'll take my chances.

THE ATTENDANT (AS DOCTOR). Come on, sir. Are you sure you don't want a blood test? It's a very good value for the money. THE HUSBAND *shakes his head.* What would you say if I threw in a free urinalysis? THE HUSBAND *shakes his head.* Maybe your taste runs toward psychiatry. Would you care to tell me anything exceptionally hilarious about your sex life? THE HUSBAND *shakes his head.*

THE ATTENDANT (AS DOCTOR), *out of character, stands up and addresses the audience.* Ladies and gentlemen, we're going to stop here with the dramatic presentation for a minute. With intermission—i.e., snack time—not too far off, we have some relevant information we'd like to impart.

In our continuing effort to even further enhance your customer experience—not conceding in the least that said experience is at present in any way defective or deficient—you will note that we have installed a recent addition to the lobby. It is a vintage Earn More electric hot-oil kettle popcorn popper wagon, agreed by all to be the never-since-matched high point of the popcorn popper wagon craft. Eleven and

three-quarters percent—that's one seventh—of the purchase price of a
giant-size box will be contributed to charity—to our favorite charity.
That will be sent right off to that charity—the Hospital for Sexual
Accidents.

Also you will find a long-time feature of the theater: an Old
Tyme—that's "time" with a Y instead of an I—that's T-Y-M-E—an Old
Tyme commercial peanut grinder to produce peanut butter. I will not
reveal that this industrial-grade machine was acquired by a lucky chance
for an absurd fifty dollars from a GNC store when it discontinued sales
of freshly ground peanut butter. Salted or unsalted, your choice. Smooth
only, of course. It is not true that you should consider supplying your
own container because the plastic container supplied is extremely fragile.
None of the reports of embarrassing accidents has been verified.

Thank you for your time, and now back to the play.

He sits back down on the sofa.

THE ATTENDANT (AS DOCTOR). Say, while I'm here, I might as well show
you a thing or two I have with me that I'm quite sure will be of interest
to you.

THE HUSBAND. Don't bother. I don't want any.

THE ATTENDANT (AS DOCTOR). No bother at all, my pleasure. *He picks ups up
the doctor's bag and searches in it.* Ah. Yes. *He takes a rag from the bag.* Here's
something everybody needs. A lint rag.

THE HUSBAND. I don't want any.

THE ATTENDANT (AS DOCTOR). It's a real work-saver, sir. You can wipe the
lint from your clothes with it. *He wipes his jacket with the rag.* You can wipe
tables and chairs, drapery, furniture, walls and woodwork. You can blow
your nose with it. *He blows his nose with the rag.* You can wash with it. *He
rubs his armpit with the rag.* It's very convenient, sir. And it's as strong as
canvas. *He takes the rag in both hands.* You can't rip it no matter how hard
you try. *He rips the rag in two.*

THE HUSBAND. You ripped the rag in two.

THE ATTENDANT (AS DOCTOR). You saw that? *He tosses the rag away.* As I say,
it's very strong. Would you like to buy one? *He searches in the bag.* Ah. Here's
the clincher. *He takes a small tool from the bag.* This is an all-purpose tool. Here

of course is the corkscrew. Here's a saw. A punch. A reamer. Here's a pair of scissors. Knife-blade, of course. This is a wrench.

THE HUSBAND. Hey. You cut yourself with that. You're bleeding.

THE ATTENDANT (AS DOCTOR). No, I didn't, sir. It's nothing. A nick. *A red liquid drips from the end of his finger.* This is a little pair of pliers. Here's a shovel. Here's a crane. Here's—

THE HUSBAND. You're bleeding all over the place.

THE ATTENDANT (AS DOCTOR) *holds out his hand. A red liquid flows from the end of his finger.* Nonsense. *He puts his hand in the pocket of his jacket. A red stain appears on the jacket.* I can give you a very good price on this, sir. Are you sure you wouldn't like to take it? Can you really afford to pass it up?

He pauses and clears his throat. Well, sir, much as I'd like to stay here and give you even more of my invaluable commercial counsel, I'm afraid I have to go now. Do you hear that bell? *A short pause. A bell rings.* That's another of my customers signaling me that he or she requires my invaluable services. *He looks at the stain on his jacket. As if out of character.* Man, doesn't the prop guy *love* this. *Back in character.* Anyone got a Band-Aid?

He goes to THE WIFE, *takes a call bell small bell from a pocket and puts it on the end table.* A bell for you too, ma'am. When the time comes just ring it and I'll be here in nothing flat—Johnny-on-the-spot. I did tell you, didn't I, that one of my aliases is John? *Thinking of something.* Oh, but excuse me. Your husband's name is John, isn't it? The name must be repulsive to you.

He walks swiftly stage left. He halts near the edge of the stage. He turns and faces THE HUSBAND *and* THE WIFE. Incidentally, if you happen to see the end of my finger lying around here anywhere, would you be kind enough to pick it up and save it for me? We modern surgeons perform modern miracles in the reattachment of severed digits, limbs—*(he pauses briefly)*—and organs. He walks swiftly off stage.

#

The Arrival

There is an interval.

THE HUSBAND *looks closely at his watch. He stands up and begins to pace to and fro. He wears a very anxious expression and makes nervous gestures. He wrings his hands, passes his hand through his hair, clears his throat and folds and unfolds his arms. He halts, against looks closely at his watch and continues to pace anxiously to and from. He makes more nervous gestures. Suddenly he halts, takes a deep breath, exhales audibly and continues to pace.*

THE WIFE. *Sarcastically.* Are you expecting something? . . . Or someone?

THE HUSBAND *pays no attention to her. He bites his fingernails. He thrusts his hands into his pockets and pulls them out. He coughs. He adjusts his tie, collar and jacket.*

THE WIFE. Bear up. You can take it. It won't be so bad. There's nothing to worry about. It'll all be over in a few minutes. You'll hardly feel a thing.

THE HUSBAND *pays no attention to her. He paces very swiftly, clenching and unclenching his hands, passing his hand through his hair, shaking his head, and coughing and grimacing nervously.*

THE WIFE *picks up the bell from the end table and rings it.*

THE HUSBAND *starts violently and halts. He clutches his abdomen and screws up his face into a look of great pain. He begins to stagger about.* THE WIFE *looks unconcerned. In a low agonized voice.* Ah! . . . happen . . . soon . . . happen . . . no . . . happen . . . ah! . . . no . . . about to . . . no . . . happen . . . ah! . . . . no . . . terrible . . . happen . . . soon . . . ah! . . . happen . . . no . . . horrible . . . ah! . . . catastrophe . . . damn! . . . ah! THE WIFE *rings the bell again. A loud knocking is heard at the door in the back wall. He starts and staggers more and more unsteadily.* Ah! . .. happen . . . now . . . happen . . . no . . . awful . . . now . . . ah? . . . happen . . . no . . . . dreadful . . . ah? . . . disaster . . . damn! . . . . ah! *He staggers against the sofa and teeters over it.* Pain . . . faint . . . now . . . very faint . . . very, very faint . . . very, very, very faint . . . *extremely* faint . . . ah! *He collapses onto the sofa.* Faint . . . die . . . pain . . . faint . . . ah! . . . die . . . now . . . now . . . die . . . die . . die . .. die . . . dead . . . ah! *He lies still.*

THE WIFE *rings the bell again.*

#

THE ATTENDANT (AS DOCTOR) *comes on slowly from the right. He walks to the recliner. With mock perplexity.* Do you hear a bell, ma'am? I keep thinking I hear a bell.

THE WIFE *holds up the bell in front of his face and rings it.* I *do* hear a bell. *He suddenly smiles and chuckles.* No. I was just kidding. I heard it all the time. I came as fast as I could—that is, I came as fast as you could reasonably expect me to. I have to explain that I have a reputation for flagrant impromptitude—a reputation, let me hasten to add, that I thoroughly deserve. *There is again a loud knocking at the door to the back wall. He turns towards the door and notices* THE HUSBAND *lying on the sofa. Flatly.* My goodness. What's happened here? Excuse me, ma'am. *He goes to* THE HUSBAND *and bends over him.* Hmm. Now isn't this something. Hmm. It looks like he might be dead. *He reaches inside* THE HUSBAND's *jacket for* THE HUSBAND's *wallet.*

THE DIRECTOR *manipulates the phonograph. There is a very loud sound of ruffles and flourishes, anthems, marches, drum rolls and circus tunes.*

THE ATTENDANT (AS DOCTOR) *withdraws his empty hand from under* THE HUSBAND's *jacket and stands watching* THE DIRECTOR.

THE DIRECTOR *stands up and puts on a fixed, exaggerated smile. He raises his arm and turns and faces in one direction and then another in an exaggeration of the manner of a circus performer about to attempt a feat of skill. He descends the ladder, flourishing his arm. He struts downstage, holds up his arms and turns this way and that, continuing to smile exaggeratedly. He dances upstage.* THE DIRECTOR *and* THE ATTENDANT (AS DOCTOR) *walk side by side to the stairs at the back wall. They step side-by-side up the stairs. They stand on either side of the door.* The Directors *stands with arms outstretched towards the door.* THE ATTENDANT (AS DOCTOR) *takes an oversized key from his pocket and "unlocks" the door with it. The flourishes risein a crescendo and stops.* THE ATTENDANT (AS DOCTOR) *opens the door a little way and puts his hand behind it. After a few seconds he withdraws his hand from behind the door.* THE ATTENDANT (AS DOCTOR). There's nobody there.

A foot emerges from behind the door.

THE ATTENDANT (AS DOCTOR) *attempts to close the door. He closes it on the foot.*

He looks at the foot. What's this? *He again opens the door a little way and puts his head behind it. He withdraws his head.* No wonder I didn't see it. It's only a child.

THE INFANT *flings the door all the way open. It bangs against the wall. He steps onto the top step. He looks around. He rubs his eyes with his fists.*

The actors freeze.

There is an interval.

With a downward motion of his baton, THE DIRECTOR *signals for the lights to go down.*

Seven or eight seconds later, the lights go down.

The Arrival

ACT TWO

The Arrival

#

The lights go up.
The actors are motionless in the postures they froze in at the end of Act One.
THE ATTENDANT (AS DOCTOR) *closes the door, locks it with the key and puts the key in his pocket.*

There is the loud music of a march. THE ATTENDANT (AS DOCTOR) *takes* THE INFANT's *hand. As they descend the stairs,* THE DIRECTOR, *in front of them, prances backwards down the stairs. He waves his arms and stretches them toward* THE INFANT *in an exaggeration of the manner of a person eliciting applause for a stage-performer.* THE ATTENDANT (AS DOCTOR) *and* THE INFANT *walk a short distance downstage and stand watching* THE DIRECTOR *prance about. The flowing music of strings and woods is heard.* THE DIRECTOR *hops, pirouettes and waves his arms in a parade of ballet. He ascends the ladder, waving his free arm. He manipulates the phonograph and the music stops. He makes elaborate bows, flaunting his cap, holding out his arms and throwing kisses at the audience. After some time he sits down. Suddenly the smile disappears from his face.*

THE INFANT. Well, here I am. I've finally arrived. *As if brushing something from his arm and then shaking it off his hand.* Here I am—all blood and gore, slime and shit. . . . Yuck. I don't think I'll do that again.

THE ATTENDANT (AS DOCTOR) looks at THE HUSBAND, who lies still on the sofa. To THE INFANT. I'll be with you in just a moment. I'm occupied with another patient right now. Wait here.

THE ATTENDANT (AS DOCTOR) *walks to* THE HUSBAND *and again puts his hand inside* THE HUSBAND's *jacket, reaching for* THE HUSBAND's *wallet.* THE HUSBAND *stirs and pushes at* THE ATTENDANT (AS DOCTOR)'s *hand.*

THE ATTENDANT (AS DOCTOR). Damn! Alive! *He moves quickly to seize* THE

71

HUSBAND's *wallet.*

THE HUSBAND sits up. They push and slap at each other's hands. THE HUSBAND pushes THE ATTENDANT (AS DOCTOR)'s hands away and folds his arms on his chest.

THE ATTENDANT (AS DOCTOR). Hey. I thought you were dead, sir. What's the big idea of waking up like this before I've stolen money? your THE HUSBAND *glares at him. He shrugs his shoulders.* Oh well, all in good time. *Suddenly* THE DIRECTOR *puts on an exaggerated smile, stands up, bows flamboyantly several times, throws kisses to the audience and sits down. The smile abruptly disappears from his face.*

THE HUSBAND. *Speaking to the audience as if out of character. Indicating* THE DIRECTOR. Can you beat that guy? There's hams and there's hams, but he takes the cake. And corny! . . . Well, you see for yourself. . . . *He looks in passing at* THE INFANT. *To himself.* Ugly kid. I wonder whose it is?

THE ATTENDANT (AS DOCTOR) *takes the key from his pocket and holds it out to* THE HUSBAND. Here's the key, sir.

THE HUSBAND. What? Key? I don't want any key.

THE ATTENDANT (AS DOCTOR). Take it, sir.

THE HUSBAND. I said I don't want it. What do I need a key for? Keep it yourself.

THE WIFE. *Out of character.* The script says you're supposed to take the key. Take it. It's supposed to be a symbol.

THE HUSBAND. *Speaking as if out of character.* A cymbal? He holds the key by one end, raps it with a knuckle and holds it up to his ear. It don't sound like a cymbal to me. *He looks closely at the key.* That's a goddam *key* if I ever seen one. *He takes the key, shrugs his shoulders and puts the key in his pocket. Indicating* THE DIRECTOR, *scornfully.* And he thinks he's a genius.

\#

THE INFANT *wears a bewildered expression. He squints and turns around, looking around curiously.* THE ATTENDANT (AS DOCTOR) *takes his arm.*

THE INFANT *shades his eyes with his hand.* It's awfully bright out here.

THE ATTENDANT (AS DOCTOR). Come on. *He pulls* THE INFANT *after him to the sofa. He sets* THE INFANT *on his knee and examines him as doctor examines a patient.* So it's a boy, is it?

THE INFANT. That's clear enough.

THE ATTENDANT (AS DOCTOR). *To* THE HUSBAND. It's a boy.

THE HUSBAND. What is?

THE ATTENDANT (AS DOCTOR) *continues to examine* THE INFANT. Well, let's see what we have here. . . . The feet and ears are too large. . . . But the nose makes up for it: it's too small. . . . A receding chin . . . but protruding ears. *He draws up the corners of* THE INFANT*'s mouth.* A weak smile—. Oh look: it has a tooth. A weak but toothy smile.

THE INFANT. Are you looking for something in particular?

THE ATTENDANT (AS DOCTOR). Deficiencies, anomalies, abnormalities, deformities.

THE INFANT. Deformities? What if I should have a deformity?

THE ATTENDANT (AS DOCTOR). The customer might be dissatisfied.

THE INFANT. The customer?

THE ATTENDANT (AS DOCTOR). The . . . the patron . . . the client . . . the purchaser . . . the buyer. *Indicating* THE HUSBAND. He might complain that the purchased product was imperfect. Customers are sometimes very fussy that way. Prices might have to be slashed. My numbers might suffer.

THE INFANT. I really don't think I have any deformities.

THE ATTENDANT (AS DOCTOR). Let's hope not for my sake. *He examines* THE INFANT *further.*

THE INFANT. What do you see?

THE ATTENDANT (AS DOCTOR). Apparently nothing wrong on the outside. But then of course there's the matter of the inside, which of course may very well be defective in some way. *He pulls* THE INFANT *from his knee and puts his ear to* THE INFANT*'s chest.*

THE HUSBAND. You don't need me for this, do you? I don't have to stay here for this, do I? I'll just be going along now. *He stands up.*

THE ATTENDANT (AS DOCTOR). *Firmly.* Nonsense, sir. I haven't presented yet.

THE HUSBAND. "Presented"?

THE ATTENDANT (AS DOCTOR). The bill. If you went now I wouldn't be able to present you with the bill.

THE HUSBAND. That's right. . . . I'm going.

THE ATTENDANT (AS DOCTOR). Nonsense, sir. *He looks sternly at* THE
HUSBAND. THE HUSBAND *reluctantly sits down.*

He again puts his ear to THE INFANT's *chest. He thumps* THE INFANT's *chest.*
He thumps it harder.

THE INFANT. *What do you hear?*

THE ATTENDANT (AS DOCTOR) *removes his ear from* THE INFANT's *chest and*
frowns. Umph. That's funny.

THE INFANT. What's the matter?

THE ATTENDANT (AS DOCTOR). I don't hear anything. *He puts his ear to* THE
INFANT's *chest again and thumps* THE INFANT's *chest harder.*

THE INFANT. If you hit me any harder you'll hear the sound of breaking
bones.

THE ATTENDANT (AS DOCTOR) *puzzles.* I don't understand it. . . . *Ahah!*
That's it! *Explaining.* I'm deaf in that ear. *He puts the other ear to* THE
INFANT's *chest and thumps* THE INFANT's *chest.*

THE INFANT. Is there anything wrong in there?

THE ATTENDANT (AS DOCTOR). I can't give you a definite answer to that
question without learning more about the practice of medicine. But I'd
say on the basis of this hasty look-over that all the necessary organs seem
to be present. . . . For business purposes I'll assume that they're more or
less in working order.

Now to test the intelligence. This won't take long: the customer
demands very little in this department.

Assume for the sake of arithmetic that a man and his wife have five
children and then they have twins. How many children to they have
now?

THE INFANT *hesitates.*

THE ATTENDANT (AS DOCTOR). Well? . . . Come on. That's not so difficult.

THE INFANT. Siamese twins?

THE ATTENDANT (AS DOCTOR). Oh. . . . I see your point. . . . No, ordinary
twins.

THE INFANT. Seven.

THE HUSBAND *yawns.* I'm tired of all this. *To* THE ATTENDANT (AS

DOCTOR). Have you got another bed around here someplace. I'd just as soon go to sleep and forget all about this business.

THE ATTENDANT (AS DOCTOR). To THE HUSBAND. Please, sir. Can't you pay attention. I'm putting on this act entirely for your benefit. *He pauses. Correcting himself.* Well, to be strictly accurate, for *my* benefit. But please pay attention anyway. *To* THE INFANT. Now suppose four of the children starve to death and the couple has quadruplets but only half the babies live and then the couple has triplets and then six of the children are beaten to death and then the couple has twins again. *Quickly anticipating* THE INFANT's *question.* Ordinary twins. How many children does the couple have now?

THE INFANT. None.

THE ATTENDANT (AS DOCTOR). *Puzzled.* None? No. They have *four.*

THE INFANT. Yes. One was run over by a freight train, two committed suicide and one was drafted.

THE ATTENDANT (AS DOCTOR) *puzzles.* Umm. What a curiously morbid mind you have!

A bell rings offstage.

THE HUSBAND *starts.* Hey. There's a bell. That's one of your customers. You've got to go now. Don't worry: I promise I won't leave without paying. I'd never think of doing such a thing. THE ATTENDANT (AS DOCTOR) *is silent and does not move.* Didn't you hear that bell ring?

THE ATTENDANT (AS DOCTOR). Certainly I heard it ring, sir. You mustn't suppose I'm as deaf as you occasionally find it convenient to be.

THE HUSBAND. *With a show of excitement.* Well? What are you waiting for? It might be an emergency!

THE ATTENDANT (AS DOCTOR). *Calm.* In fact there's a very good chance that it *is,* sir.

THE HUSBAND. Excitedly. You've got to go now! You've got to hurry! THE ATTENDANT (AS DOCTOR) *shakes his head.* But you can't make your patients wait!

THE ATTENDANT (AS DOCTOR). Oh my! You're quite an actor, sir. Your concern sounds almost genuine. . . No harm in making them wait, sir. It's for the good of their souls: teaches them patience in the face of neglect.

Besides, sir, we can't spoil them, can we now?

#

THE ATTENDANT (AS DOCTOR). *With a show of enthusiasm. Like a salesman.*
Well, sir! I am happy to be able to report to you that after thorough-
going superficial inspection I can confidently declare that we have here a
healthy bumping, bounding, jumping, thumping, bouncing baby boy! *He
bounces* THE INFANT *roughly on his knee.*
THE INFANT. Hey, easy, Trigger. You'll dent the merchandise.
THE ATTENDANT (AS DOCTOR) *pulls* THE INFANT *from his knee and holds him
facing* THE HUSBAND. Yes, sir! Wonderful infant! He tickles THE
INFANT's chin. Isn't it cute. *Talking baby talk.* Ba-ba cwutey eenay-teeney-
weeney ba-ba. Smilems ba-ba?
THE INFANT. C'mon. . . . Don't talk like a moron. You're making a spectacle
of yourself.
THE ATTENDANT (AS DOCTOR). Dinkums-winkums dolly-wolly coochy-
wouchy itchy-boo.
THE INFANT *shrugs.* Suit yourself, dude.
THE ATTENDANT (AS DOCTOR). *To* THE HUSBAND. *Isn't this just the cutest little
ba-ba you ever did see?*
THE HUSBAND. Ba-ba.
THE ATTENDANT (AS DOCTOR). Yes. The little ba-ba here. You mean you
don't *see* the little ba-ba here? *He pauses.* I mean the baby, of course.
THE HUSBAND. Oh, the baby. . . *Perplexed.* What baby?
THE ATTENDANT (AS DOCTOR). There is only *one* baby here. The baby
standing right her.
THE HUSBAND. I don't see any baby.
THE ATTENDANT (AS DOCTOR). Well . . . what would you call it, sir? A babe .
. . an infant . . . a child . . . a youngster . . . .
THE HUSBAND. A minor . . . a juvenile . . . an immature person . . . .
THE ATTENDANT (AS DOCTOR). *Enthusiastic.* Yes! Exactly! An immature
person. Of course you see the immature person standing right here.
THE HUSBAND. No.

THE ATTENDANT (AS DOCTOR). *To* THE WIFE. Surely *you* see the immature person standing right here?

THE WIFE. Of course.

THE ATTENDANT (AS DOCTOR). *To* THE HUSBAND. But you don't?

THE HUSBAND. No.

THE ATTENDANT (AS DOCTOR). *Hmmmm (ponders with his hand at his chin).* Now isn't that peculiar . . . . It's . . . it's . . . strange. . . . It's . . . astonishing . . . . Is it . . . *psychosomatic?*

THE HUSBAND. I can't help it. . . . I caught it in Tijuana.

THE ATTENDANT (AS DOCTOR). My wild guess is that, incredible as it may seem to us normal people, you are psychologically unable to recognize the existence of this infant because for some reason—probably having to do with money—you don't *want* to recognize its existence. That kinda wraps it up, don't you think.

THE HUSBAND. That doesn't seem very incredible to me. I could have told you that. *He pauses.* But I won't.

THE ATTENDANT (AS DOCTOR). *Abruptly all alert. He sniffs as if he smells something. He makes a face and pinches his nose. He looks* at THE INFANT. *He frowns and pushes* THE INFANT *away. To* THE HUSBAND, *indicating* THE INFANT. I know you don't *see* it, sir, but don't tell me you don't *smell* it.

THE HUSBAND. That's me. I farted.

THE ATTENDANT (AS DOCTOR) *instantly takes his hand from his nose, and assumes a blank expression.* Oh, excuse *me.* I don't smell anything. The customer is always right and never, never, *never* farts. . . . *He smiles.* That's another clever motto I made up, sir.

He considers. Now let's see. You'd don't *see* this immature person. I don't *smell* you. Perhaps you would *feel* it punch you. *To* THE INFANT. Punch him hard.

THE INFANT *punches* THE HUSBAND *in the face.* THE HUSBAND, *reacting instinctively, moves to strike* THE INFANT *with his fist.* THE ATTENDANT (AS DOCTOR) *grabs his arm.*

THE ATTENDANT (AS DOCTOR). *With mock astonishment.* Sir! You don't want to *injure* this immature person, do you?

THE HUSBAND. *Controlling himself. Sullenly.* No, I don't. *Suddenly losing control again, shouting. I want to kill it!*

THE ATTENDANT (AS DOCTOR). And of course you didn't feel it punch you just now.

THE HUSBAND. *Controlling himself again.* No.

THE ATTENDANT (AS DOCTOR). *With his hand to his chin.* Now isn't that interesting . . . . I'd write your case up in the medical journal if it wasn't far too common to be of anyone's interest. .

#

THE HUSBAND *suddenly jumps to his feet and dashes to the left and off stage.*

THE ATTENDANT (AS DOCTOR). *Shouting after him.* Sir! Come back, sir! Come back! *Calm, to* THE WIFE. Ma'am. I'm afraid you'll have to excuse me. Would you, please? Your husband's precipitous, ill-conceived and ultimately futile bolting-like-a-scared-rabbit-in-order-to-avoid-payment makes it necessary for me to go and nab him now.

THE WIFE. Go right ahead.

THE ATTENDANT (AS DOCTOR). Thank you, ma'am. *He stands up and begins to walk to the right. He halts and faces* THE WIFE. Wait. He takes a paper from his pocket. Maybe *you* could settle this. Maybe you have money stashed in the usual places. Show me your garter belt.

THE WIFE. I don't have any money stashed in my garter belt.

THE ATTENDANT (AS DOCTOR). Show me.

THE WIFE. Why? Don't you believe me?

THE ATTENDANT (AS DOCTOR). Yes. Show me.

THE WIFE. If you absolutely insist. She stands up and draws up her skirt above her garter belt.

THE ATTENDANT (AS DOCTOR). Higher. I can't see it. THE WIFE *draws up her skirt higher.* Higher. THE WIFE draws up her skirt still higher. There is a long pause as THE ATTENDANT (AS DOCTOR) looks at her. *Out of character.* I don't care what the critics say about this play, *I* like it. *Back in character. He walks to* THE WIFE *and looks in the bodice of her dress.* Let's look in the other usual place.

THE DIRECTOR *raps the umpire's chair shelf with the baton and shakes his head.*

The Arrival

THE ATTENDANT (AS DOCTOR) *grimaces in disappointment and turns away from* THE WIFE. *As if out of character. Indicating* THE DIRECTOR. What a kill-joy this guy is. . . . *Back in character.* Excuse me then, ma'am. *He bolts and dashes to the left and off stage...*
THE WIFE *sits down in the chair.*
There is an interval of about ten seconds.
THE ATTENDANT (AS DOCTOR) *and* THE HUSBAND *walk on from the left.*
THE ATTENDANT (AS DOCTOR) *draws* THE HUSBAND *after him by the arm.*
THE HUSBAND. How did you catch up with me?
THE ATTENDANT (AS DOCTOR). You made the mistake of running through the town of Friendship, sir.
THE HUSBAND. I did? What happened? I know. I broke a leg.
THE ATTENDANT (AS DOCTOR). *Glares at him. Disparaging.* No. You will *never* break a leg. . . . No, you got caught in their radar trap.
He draws THE HUSBAND *to the sofa and seats him. He sits down.*
A bell sounds off stage to the right.
THE HUSBAND *starts and exclaims with exaggerated fervor. A bell! A bell! A bell just rang! A bell rang! It did! I swear it did! To* THE WIFE. Didn't it ring? Tell him: a bell just rang! *To* THE ATTENDANT (AS DOCTOR). A bell just rang! That means you've got to go now! You've got to go right now! Somebody's probably about to die!
THE ATTENDANT (AS DOCTOR). *Calm.* They've lasted so far, haven't they?
The longer, louder ringing of a bell sounds.
THE ATTENDANT (AS DOCTOR). Damn it, sir. I guess I'll have to go and take that bell away from the impatient patient who's ringing it. The way he's banging it around he might break it. And they *do* cost a buck forty-nine. And that's even though they're made by cheap labor in Jersey City.
He walks to the right and walks off stage.

#

THE HUSBAND *walks swiftly to the right edge of the stage and looks around towards the right.*
THE HUSBAND. All clear.

The Arrival

THE HUSBAND *walks to the sofa and takes* THE WIFE'S *coat from it. He quickly hands it to* THE WIFE, *who puts it on. He walks to the suitcase and picks it up, with difficulty.* THE HUSBAND *and* THE WIFE *walk swiftly off right.*

After about fifteen seconds THE HUSBAND, *carrying the suitcase, and* THE WIFE *come on stage from the right walking backwards.* THE ATTENDANT (AS DOCTOR) *comes on from the right walking towards them with a menacing look. The three actors—* THE HUSBAND *and* THE WIFE *walking backwards—walk to the center of the stage and halt.*

THE HUSBAND *drops the suitcase. The very loud sound-effects thud sounds.*

But . . . but how did you know we were trying to get away? You were supposed to be occupied with another customer.

THE ATTENDANT (AS DOCTOR). *Amiable.* Oh I was, sir, I was. The desk clerk saw you running through the lobby. He tipped me off. *He smiles.* We work together.

THE HUSBAND. But we were running like mad. How did he have time to tip you off?

THE ATTENDANT (AS DOCTOR). Walkie-talkie, sir.

So you might just as well—*(he breaks off as if he thinks of something)—* except in the off chance you'd like to pay up *now—he looks questioningly at* THE HUSBAND. THE HUSBAND *shakes his head*—you might just as well sit down and make yourself comfortable as possible under the circumstances. *To* THE WIFE. Here, ma'am. Let me help you with your coat. *He helps* THE WIFE *off with her overcoat. He holds it out to* THE HUSBAND, *who is looking away.* Sir, your wife's coat, remember? THE HUSBAND *looks at him, takes the coat and hangs it on the clothes tree..* THE WIFE *sits in the recliner.* THE HUSBAND *and* THE ATTENDANT (AS DOCTOR) *sit on the sofa.*

#

THE HUSBAND *stands up.* Hey, that's a real pretty picture you got hung up on your wall over there close to the door I'm thinking of running out of.

THE ATTENDANT (AS DOCTOR). *Firmly.* Sit down, sir. You're not fooling anybody.

THE HUSBAND. I'll just meander over there and take a closer look at it. *He walks to the left edge of the stage and looks at a "picture" on the left "wall."* THE ATTENDANT (AS DOCTOR), *unobserved by him, approaches him slowly.* Who's that by? I bet that's by that fellow—what's his name?—Pizzicato.

THE ATTENDANT (AS DOCTOR). *Walking towards* THE HUSBAND. Yes, sir, that's a very valuable original reproduction. Luckily for me the man at the gallery at Woolworth's didn't recognize it as genuine paper-maché.

THE HUSBAND. *Tilting his head from side to side.* It *is* pretty, even though I don't quite see what it's supposed to be. *He points.* I can see that that's a titty, of course, but I don't really understand this other stuff. *He suddenly moves to run off left..*

THE ATTENDANT (AS DOCTOR). *Continuing to walk towards* THE HUSBAND. *Wait, sir!* THE HUSBAND *halts, continuing to look towards the left. In a pedantic tone.* Before you try to bolt, sir, notice in that painting the suggestion of motion from left to right and also the suggestion of motion from right to left, which combine to give a perfect suggestion of motionlessness, also in the lower left-hand corner the little penis made to look like a nose—or according to other critics—the little nose made to look like a penis.

THE HUSBAND. I do see that. Tell me more. *He bolts towards the left.* THE ATTENDANT (AS DOCTOR), *now near* THE HUSBAND, *immediately reaches out and catches him by the arm. He draws him to the sofa and seats him. He sits down on the sofa.*

#

THE ATTENDANT (AS DOCTOR). Let me just run over some other of this infant's stand-out selling features, sir. To THE INFANT. Go ahead and tell him. THE INFANT *is silent.* Go ahead and tell the man: what are you good for? THE INFANT is silent. Well? Haven't you got anything to say for yourself?

THE INFANT. *Rapidly, expressionlessly.* I can boondoggle whistle thongs. I can build sand castles. I can make giraffes out of buttons and paper clips.

THE ATTENDANT (AS DOCTOR). *Enthusiastic.* Wonderful! Whistle thongs! Sand castles! Giraffes! A great little production worker!

THE INFANT. I can spell "abracadabra." I can write upside down and backwards. I can type with my nose.

THE ATTENDANT (AS DOCTOR). Great! Spell! Write! Type! All important stenographic skills!

THE INFANT. I can throw skitters. I can make spitballs out of book matches. I can spit seventeen feet.

THE ATTENDANT (AS DOCTOR). Tremendous! Amazing military abilities!

THE INFANT. I can stand on one foot for five minutes. I can beat Betty Green at potsy.

THE ATTENDANT (AS DOCTOR). Splendid! Did you hear that, sir! It's a fantastic natural athlete!

THE INFANT. I can say the Gettysburg Address backwards. I can cite to the Constitution in any connection. I can talk out of three sides of my mouth at the same time.

THE ATTENDANT (AS DOCTOR). Oh my! Wonderful! It has political skills!

THE INFANT. I can tie a clove hitch. I can track Rocky mountain sheep. I can shoot a sitting duck.

THE ATTENDANT (AS DOCTOR). Marvelous! A woodsman! Very impressive.

THE INFANT. I can play *The Old Gray Mare* on my recorder. I can whistle Dixie underwater.

THE ATTENDANT (AS DOCTOR). Excellent! A musician too! It can even sing *The Star-Spangled Banner* note-perfect, sir.

THE INFANT. I can blow soap bubbles as big—

THE ATTENDANT (AS DOCTOR). *Peremptory.* That's enough. To THE HUSBAND. That'll give you some impression, sir. And of course I could go on and on.

THE INFANT. I can blow soap bubbles—

THE ATTENDANT (AS DOCTOR). *Peremptory. I said that's enough.*

#

THE ATTENDANT (AS DOCTOR) *looks around.* What's all that noise I hear?

THE HUSBAND. I don't hear anything.

THE INFANT *points at his stomach.* Here. My stomach. It means I'm starving.

THE ATTENDANT (AS DOCTOR) *puts his ear to* THE INFANT's *stomach.* I don't hear anything, either. *As if he thinks of something.* Oh. *He turns his head and puts his other ear to* THE INFANT's *stomach.* Why, it sounds like a *locomotive* in there.

THE INFANT. Do you mean the rumble, the whistle, or the hiss?

THE ATTENDANT (AS DOCTOR). All three. And the squeak.

THE INFANT. That's not me squeaking. *Pointing.* That's your air-conditioner.

THE ATTENDANT (AS DOCTOR) *listens.* Ah. So it is. . . . *Angrily.* Is that sorry machine on the fritz again! The God damned appliance man sold us a lemon! You just can't trust anybody else around here, either. . . . Hmmmm . . . We can't let this thing starve. Perhaps something in the way of milk is in order.

THE HUSBAND. Who said?

THE INFANT. Sounds good. I'll have a glass of buttermilk, please.

THE ATTENDANT (AS DOCTOR). *Looking at* THE WIFE. The fact is I'm not thinking exactly of *cow's* milk.

THE WIFE *folds her arms over her breasts.* No dice.

THE ATTENDANT (AS DOCTOR). I know it's grotesque, ma'am, but remember: it's free; it would save you money.

THE HUSBAND. *Quickly, urgently to* THE WIFE. Go ahead.

THE WIFE. *Grim.* I don't like the look of that tooth.

THE ATTENDANT (AS DOCTOR). Well, if Mother here won't cooperate milk-wise, let's see what else we've got in the foodstuffs department. . . . Ah! Here we are. *He takes an apple from the pocket of his jacket.*

THE HUSBAND. Where did you get that?

THE ATTENDANT (AS DOCTOR). It belongs to my last customer. You'll understand when you see the end of the play. *He gives* THE INFANT *the apple.* THE INFANT *begins to eat it.*

THE HUSBAND *abruptly stands up.* I'm going out now for coffee and sandwiches. What do you two want? *Rapidly.* Both with cream, one with sugar, one BLT on toast, relish, hold the mayo, small order of fries, one ham and cheese on rye, heavy on the ketchup plus one large fries and don't forget the salt—is that right? Fine. I'll be back in a sec. *He begins to*

The Arrival

walk stage left.

THE ATTENDANT (AS DOCTOR). Sit down, sir.

THE HUSBAND. Fritos?

THE ATTENDANT (AS DOCTOR) *looks sternly at* THE HUSBAND. THE HUSBAND *reluctantly returns and sits down on the sofa.*

THE ATTENDANT (AS DOCTOR). In short, sir, I think you can't help but agree with me that all-in-all this outstanding specimen of an infant is absolutely and undeniably a first-prize, blue-ribbon, best-quality, best-of-breed commodity. *He takes a paper from his pocket and hands it to* THE HUSBAND. I think—all things taken into account *(he pauses briefly)* at least twice—that you'll find my figures to be entirely unfair and unreasonable. *He hands the paper to* THE HUSBAND.

THE HUSBAND. *Looking at the paper, turning it this way and that, upside-down and over. Indicating the paper.* What's this?

THE ATTENDANT (AS DOCTOR). Please, sir. Don't pretend you don't know why I've been forcing myself to perform the loathsome task of babbling to you for the last I-don't-know-how-many hours. It's the bill, of course.

THE HUSBAND. What? I can't hear you. . . . You say this is a Christmas card? Well, merry Christmas to you, too. THE ATTENDANT (AS DOCTOR) *looks at him sternly and shakes his head. Rapidly.* I mean, you say it's a thank-you note. You're entirely welcome. THE ATTENDANT (AS DOCTOR) *shakes his head.* . . . I mean, you say it's an inter-office memo. I'll take care of it next week. THE ATTENDANT (AS DOCTOR) shakes his head. . . . I mean, you say it's a map of Foggy Bottom. *Disinterested.* Very interesting. *He tosses the paper to the floor.*

There is an interval.

THE ATTENDANT (AS DOCTOR) *glares at* THE HUSBAND *menacingly.* THE ATTENDANT (AS DOCTOR) *takes another paper from his pocket and hands it to* THE HUSBAND. THE HUSBAND *folds it in two and tosses it away as if it were a paper airplane.*

THE ATTENDANT (AS DOCTOR) *hands* THE HUSBAND *another piece paper. He crumbles it into a ball and swats it away as if he were serving a volleyball.*

THE ATTENDANT (AS DOCTOR) *hands* THE HUSBAND *another piece of paper.* THE HUSBAND *bites into it as if it were a piece of food, screws up his face as*

84

if it tasted bad and tosses it away.

THE ATTENDANT (AS DOCTOR) *hands* THE HUSBAND *another piece of paper.* THE HUSBAND *wipes his mouth with it as if it were a napkin, wipes his hands with it as if it were a [napkin or] towel, crumples it and tosses it away.* `paper. He tosses it to the floor. He sits down.*

THE ATTENDANT (AS DOCTOR) *takes a sheaf of papers from his pocket. He hands one of the papers to* THE HUSBAND. THE HUSBAND *takes it and immediately tosses it away.*

THE ATTENDANT (AS DOCTOR) *hands* THE HUSBAND *five or six of the papers one after the other.* THE HUSBAND *takes each of them, except the last, and immediately tosses it away. He holds the last paper. He frowns and grimaces. He holds the paper at his knee.*

THE HUSBAND. *With exaggerated affability.* Wonderful horrible weather we're having, isn't it? *He smiles broadly. He lets the paper drop inconspicuously from his hand.* THE ATTENDANT (AS DOCTOR) *quickly hands him another paper. He frowns.*

He looks around. He points. Look over there. THE ATTENDANT (AS DOCTOR) *looks where he points.* There's an elephant crawling up the wall. See it? *Still pointing, he tosses the paper to the floor.* THE ATTENDANT (AS DOCTOR), *still looking where* THE HUSBAND *is pointing, takes another paper from the sheaf of papers and hands it to him. He frowns.*

He crumples the paper and puts it in a pocket of his jacket. He smiles and pats the pocket. That's my trash pocket.

THE INFANT *suddenly clutches his stomach and groans loudly.* Uh! . .. hurts . . . ah! stomach . . . uh! . . . pain . .. ah! . . . stomach . . .

THE ATTENDANT (AS DOCTOR) *frowns. Concerned.* Uh-oh. What's this? *He goes to* THE INFANT *and examines his eyes, ears and teeth.*

THE INFANT. Ah! . . . hurts . . . pain . .. uh! stomach . . . ah! . . . stomach . . . .

THE HUSBAND. No baby for me, no pay for you.

THE ATTENDANT (AS DOCTOR). *To* THE HUSBAND. Good news for me, sir. My guess is that the affliction is not fatal. *He looks at* THE INFANT *groaning.* It is probably painful, however. . . . *He claps his hands and rubs them together. Smiling.* Clearly this case will require my further services.

He *pulls* THE INFANT *to the sofa. To* THE WIFE *in the recliner.* Excuse me, please, ma'am. I think we've got your trouble just about cleared up. *He indicates* THE INFANT. My next customer.

THE WIFE *gets up from the recliner and sits on the sofa.* THE INFANT *sits in the reclinerr.* THE INFANT *continues to clutch his stomach and groan.*

THE ATTENDANT (AS DOCTOR). Evidently your son is in some pain, sir.

THE HUSBAND. You exaggerate.

THE ATTENDANT (AS DOCTOR). With a salesman's manner. If I may be permitted to make a suggestion, sir, maybe I could be helpful in recommending something in the area of medication. I'm not an expert in this area, of course, but I do have some personal experience I'm willing to share..

THE HUSBAND. I'm not paying for any medication. It's only acting. It's done this before. It's trying to trick me into thinking it's sick so I'll buy it a box of its favorite black cherry jujubes.

THE ATTENDANT (AS DOCTOR). *Deliberate.* Maybe we should ask it what the matter seems to be.

THE HUSBAND. It'd only lie.

THE ATTENDANT (AS DOCTOR). I'm quite sure it'll say it feels bad and would like you to buy it medication. *To* THE INFANT. Do you feel bad?

THE INFANT. *Haltingly.* Not . . . right . . . now. I'm . . . numb. I . . . don't feel anything.

THE HUSBAND. *Quickly to* THE ATTENDANT (AS DOCTOR). That settles it. You can go now.

THE ATTENDANT (AS DOCTOR) *turns to the end table, rolls back his cuffs and touches some of the medicine bottles. Rubbing his hands together.* Now then, I'll just whip up something mouth-watering.

THE HUSBAND *slides off the sofa onto his hands and knees. He makes a barking sound.*

THE ATTENDANT (AS DOCTOR). *Flatly to* THE WIFE. What's wrong with your husband, ma'am?

THE WIFE. He thinks he's a dog. He gets that way sometimes when his problems overwhelm him.

THE HUSBAND *begins to crawl towards the right.* THE ATTENDANT (AS DOCTOR) *walks quickly to him.* THE HUSBAND *growls at* THE ATTENDANT (AS

86

DOCTOR). *He snaps at* THE ATTENDANT (AS DOCTOR)'s *foot.* THE
ATTENDANT (AS DOCTOR) *evades him. He scampers on his hands and knees stage
left.* THE ATTENDANT (AS DOCTOR) *quickly seizes him by his jacket collar.*
THE ATTENDANT (AS DOCTOR). You're a pretty slow dog, sir. Next time
  you'd better think you're a greyhound. *He pulls* THE HUSBAND *on his hand
  and knees toward the sofa.*
THE HUSBAND. Hey. You're choking me.
THE ATTENDANT (AS DOCTOR). Jeez. A talking dog, yet.
  THE ATTENDANT (AS DOCTOR) *seats* THE HUSBAND *on the sofa, hands him
a paper and walks to the end table.*
  THE HUSBAND *holds up the paper in one hand, strikes it with his other fist. It
drops to the floor..*
THE ATTENDANT (AS DOCTOR) *picks up one medicine bottle and then another. To*
  THE INFANT, *who continues to clutch his stomach and groan.* Shall we start with
  something pink? *He recklessly pours from one of the bottles into a glass, holds up
  the glass and looks at it.* Pretty color, isn't it? Looks pretty enough to drink,
  doesn't it? I think this stuff tastes like apricots. Delicious. *He hands the
  glass to* THE INFANT. THE INFANT *drinks the liquid.*
THE INFANT groans and grimaces, clutching his stomach. Uh! . . . stomach . .
  . ah! . . . stomach . . .
THE ATTENDANT (AS DOCTOR) *considers.* Hmm. *Tentatively.* Perhaps
  something for the *stomach* . . . *He searches among the bottles.* I don't see— Ah.
  He picks up a bottle. Here we are. *Looking at the label of the bottle.* I think it
  says something about stomach here . . .
THE HUSBAND. *Suspicious.* What is it?
THE ATTENDANT (AS DOCTOR). *Looking more closely at the label.* I don't know,
  sir, but whatever it is, it certainly does have a long name. . . . We'll use it
  anyway.
THE HUSBAND. Why?
THE ATTENDANT (AS DOCTOR). *Indicating the label.* My Uncle Zeke owns the
  company. *He pours from the bottle into a glass and hands the glass to* THE
  INFANT. THE INFANT *drinks the liquid.*
  THE ATTENDANT (AS DOCTOR) *picks up another bottle and is about to pour
from it into another glass.*

87

THE HUSBAND. What's that for?

THE ATTENDANT (AS DOCTOR). For what ails you. *He chuckles loudly.* No, just joking, sir. . . . Let's see. *He looks at the label.* It says it's for neuralgia.

THE HUSBAND. Neuralgia! He doesn't have neuralgia!

THE ATTENDANT (AS DOCTOR). Of course he doesn't have neuralgia. *He pauses.* But how do *you* know it doesn't have neuralgia? You're not a highly qualified medical personnel. He pours from the bottle into a glass.

THE HUSBAND. Hey. You're giving it too much.

THE ATTENDANT (AS DOCTOR). In the business world, sir, there is no such thing as too much of a good thing.

THE HUSBAND. *Indicating the bottles.* You won't catch me paying for any of this garbage—not necessary.

THE ATTENDANT (AS DOCTOR) .*Not* necessary. But it *is* expensive. *He hands the glass* to THE INFANT, *who drinks the liquid.*

THE HUSBAND *abruptly leaps to his feet. Shouting. Atomic attack!* . . . *Atomic attack!* . . . *Atomic attack!* . . . *Everybody hit the fall-out shelter!* . . . *Bring your chips! He runs off stage to the left.*

THE ATTENDANT (AS DOCTOR). *Calm.* Excuse me again, ma'am. I'm afraid I'll have to go and corral your hubby again.

THE WIFE. You're excused.

THE ATTENDANT (AS DOCTOR). Thank you indeed, ma'am. *He abruptly bolts and dashes off stage to the left.*

There is an interval of about fifteen seconds.

They come back on from stage from the left. THE ATTENDANT (AS DOCTOR) *pulls* THE HUSBAND *after him by a sleeve of his jacket.*

THE HUSBAND. How did you catch me?

THE ATTENDANT (AS DOCTOR). You were headed back here all by yourself. You didn't stay at the fall-out shelter.

THE HUSBAND. Really? Why's that?

THE ATTENDANT (AS DOCTOR). They were charging admission.

He pulls THE HUSBAND *to the sofa, seats him, hands him a sheet of paper, and steps to the end table.*

THE HUSBAND *fans himself with the paper and tosses it away..*

THE ATTENDANT (AS DOCTOR) *rummages through the bottles, picks up one of them and smells its contents.* Umm. He pours from the bottle into a glass and sips

The Arrival

the liquid. Umm. Not bad. *He drinks again.* Umm. Very good. I wonder
how this good stuff got out here. *To* THE HUSBAND. *Would you care for a
little drink, sir? He pours from the bottle into another glass.*
THE HUSBAND. Now wait. I'm not paying—
THE ATTENDANT (AS DOCTOR). What'll it be? Water or soda? *He picks up a
jar from among the paraphernalia. Indicating the jar.* Olive? Onion? *He picks up
another jar.* Cherry? *He picks up another jar.* Prune? . ... *Straight? He hands* THE
HUSBAND *the glass.* A little drink between very close business associates.
And we *are* very close business associates, aren't we sir? You're the buyer
. .. the customer . . . the sucker, and I'm the seller . . . the chiseler. *He
smiles broadly.*
    A toast, sir. To your wife. May she have twenty more babies—
THE HUSBAND *spews out the liquid he is drinking and coughs at length.*
THE ATTENDANT (AS DOCTOR). What is it, sir? . . . Oh, that's right, you're
the one with the soft brain that's morbidly sensitive to a certain subject,
aren't you? Yes, maybe I should be more careful not to touch that sore
topic of yours. . . . To us, then, And in particular and to put it better, to
me. *They drink.*
    Taking a deep breath and exhaling audibly. Expansively. Ah. What better
way to while away the idle hours of the day than by drinking in the
company of a close business associate—at his expense.
THE HUSBAND. *Indicating* THE INFANT. Now we'll ask it whether all that
medicine you gave it made it feel any better.
THE ATTENDANT (AS DOCTOR). *Quickly.* That's not necessary, sir. I can *see*
that it feels tons better.
THE HUSBAND. It looks just the same to me.
THE ATTENDANT (AS DOCTOR). *Pompous.* The effects of the practitioner's art
are often not immediately apparent to the unpracticed eye of the layman
. . . *(to himself, in a barely audible voice)* . . . luckily for the practitioner.
THE HUSBAND. *To* THE INFANT. Do you feel any better?
THE INFANT. Well—
THE ATTENDANT (AS DOCTOR). *Quickly interrupting. Emphatically to* THE
HUSBAND. Beware of subjective judgments, sir!
THE INFANT. I feel much better, thank you.

THE ATTENDANT (AS DOCTOR). What! It feels *better? He puzzles, his hand at his chin.* Incredible. . . . How could that have happened? *Shrugging it off.* Oh well, these things happen . . . Sometimes good things happen. *He pauses briefly.* I guess.

THE HUSBAND *stands up. He puts his thumbs in his belt and swaggers around with a*

show of self-assurance. All right. All right. I've had just about enough of this pussyfooting around. Asuccessful businessman like me doesn't have time to waste. *He points at* THE ATTENDANT (AS DOCTOR). I'm not going to pull any punches with you: I'm telling you right here and now, face-to-face, straight out, man-to-man, what I think of you and your God damned bill. I don't *want* to pay your God damned bill and I'm not *going* to pay your God damned bill. There: I said it and I meant it and you can take that or put it in your pipe smoke it. *He swaggers to the left. He abruptly bolts and dashes to the left and dashes off stage.*

THE ATTENDANT (AS DOCTOR). *To* THE WIFE. Excuse me once again, ma'am. It's your husband again.

THE WIFE. Certainly. Go right ahead.

THE ATTENDANT (AS DOCTOR). Thank you, ma'am. *He steps to the left. He abruptely bolts and dashes to the left and dashes off stage.*

A pause of about ten seconds. THE ATTENDANT (AS DOCTOR) *and* THE HUSBAND *come on from stage left.* THE ATTENDANT (AS DOCTOR) *pulls* THE HUSBAND *after him by the arm.*

THE HUSBAND. I didn't think you'd ever catch up with me. Everything seemed to be going so well.

THE ATTENDANT (AS DOCTOR). Your second stage failed to ignite, sir. You fell back into the Atlantic.

THE ATTENDANT (AS DOCTOR) *hands* THE HUSBAND *a piece of paper.* THE HUSBAND *holds it between his lips.* THE HUSBAND *takes the handkerchief from the pocket of his jacket. He rings water from it. He tosses it away. He folds the paper into quarters. He puts it in the pocket of his jacket as if it were the handkerchief. He adjusts it and pats it. He smiles.*

THE ATTENDANT (AS DOCTOR) *pauses.* Well, sir, you're probably wondering by this time how this is going to turn out.

THE HUSBAND *Out of character.* No, I've acted this play lots of times. I know how it's going to turn out.

THE ATTENDANT (AS DOCTOR). *Menacing.* Of course there's only one way it *could* turn out.

THE HUSBAND. *Out of character. Considers for a moment.* I don't think so. It could be a worse play and I could conventionally commit suicide at the end. THE ATTENDANT (AS DOCTOR) *hands* THE HUSBAND *a piece of paper.* THE HUSBAND *walks to and fro. He frowns and handles the piece of paper.* THE HUSBAND *halts. He looks at the bell on the end table. He holds up his finger as if he has an idea. Unobserved by* THE ATTENDANT (AS DOCTOR), *he quickly picks up the bell land puts it in his pocket.*
During the following conversation he rolls the paper into a narrow cylinder. He sucks on the end of it as if it were a cigar. He blows out the "smoke." He tosses the paper away.

THE HUSBAND. *Shrewd.* Say, excuse me a minute, will you. *He steps to the right.*

THE ATTENDANT (AS DOCTOR). Where do you think you're going, sir?

THE HUSBAND. *Abruptly embarrassed.* Uh . . . you know . . . uh . . . all the coffee I drank . . . uh . . . while I was waiting for it to arrive.

THE ATTENDANT (AS DOCTOR). *Suspicious.* You wouldn't be trying to get away Scot-free again, would you? Is this a trick? Are you lying? Are you lying about having to go pee-pee?

THE HUSBAND. *Innocent.* No, I'm not. Anyone would feel very guilty about lying about that, including even myself.

THE ATTENDANT (AS DOCTOR) *frowns.* Just to make sure, I'll go with you.

THE HUSBAND. No, no . . . you . . . uh . . . you can't do that.

THE ATTENDANT (AS DOCTOR). *Stern.* Why not?

THE HUSBAND. *Tries to think of a reason.* Well . . . uh . . . I . . . for one reason . . . uh . . . for another reason . . . uh . . . I . . . uh . . . well, let me see . . . I couldn't do it with somebody watching.

THE ATTENDANT (AS DOCTOR). *Stern.* Why not?

THE HUSBAND. *Tries to think of a reason.* Well . . . uh . . . because . . . uh . . . because . . . uh . . . you'd make me nervous.

THE ATTENDANT (AS DOCTOR). *Abruptly persuaded.* Oh *well.* In *that* case, fine, you go right ahead.

THE HUSBAND *walks to the right and walks off stage.*

THE WIFE. *Incredulous.* And you *believed* that?

THE ATTENDANT (AS DOCTOR). Let me just quote you a motto I made up in this connection. *Reciting.* "The truth is sometimes pretty improbable." For instance, who'd believe *I* was possible?

A bell rings offstage.

THE ATTENDANT (AS DOCTOR). Excuse me, ma'am. I'd better go. *Grave.* That sounds like a certain very rich widow I'm really quite concerned about.

THE WIFE. Which is to say you are concerned about her money.

THE ATTENDANT (AS DOCTOR). No only. She's a hellava squeeze. *He walks to the right and walks off stage, downstage from the counter.*

There is an interval.

THE HUSBAND *comes on stage from the right, downstage from the counter. He smiles broadly and holds up the bell.* .

THE WIFE. *Flatly.* You rang the bell just now. THE HUSBAND *nods, smiling broadly.* To make him think that another of his customers rang for him. THE HUSBAND *nods again.* To get him out of the room. THE HUSBAND *nods again.* So we can get away Scot-free. THE HUSBAND *nods again. Pointing to the right.* Through the *back* door. THE HUSBAND *nods again.* Naturally, some tricky, despicable deception like that was to be expected of you sooner or later. THE HUSBAND *nods again.*

THE HUSBAND *puts the bell on the end table.. He walks swiftly to the right edge of the stage, upstage from the counter. He looks offstage.* All clear. *He walks to the clothes trees and takes* THE WIFE's *coat. He walks to* THE WIFE *and hands it to her.* THE WIFE *puts the coat on. He walks to the suitcase and picks it up with great difficulty.*

THE WIFE *takes* THE INFANT's *hand.* Come on. Let's go.

THE INFANT *draws his hand away.* I'd rather not. I'll wait here for your inevitable imminent return. I don't see any reason to exert myself on behalf of another fruitless attempt at flight.

THE WIFE. We have no intention to be back here.

THE INFANT. *Contemplative.* Yes. . . . In life intention is no match for life.

THE WIFE. Come on now, you little bundle of joy.

THE INFANT. *Relenting.* Well . . . okay. *He holds out his hand for* THE WIFE *to take. . . . .* But my self-concept is not that of a *bundle* of any description.

THE HUSBAND *and* THE WIFE, *with* THE INFANT *in tow, walk swiftly off stage to the right, upstage from the counter..*

There is an interval of about ten seconds.

THE HUSBAND, *carrying the suitcase with great difficulty,* THE WIFE, *and* THE INFANT *come on stage from the right walking backwards. The come on stage in the order opposite to the order in which they went off stage. They are followed on stage by* THE ATTENDANT (AS DOCTOR) *walking threateningly toward them. They halt at the center of the stage.*

THE HUSBAND *drops the bags.* But . . . but . . . how—

THE ATTENDANT (AS DOCTOR). When I quickly discovered that none of my customers had rung for me I concluded at once— incidentally, I'm extremely shrewd—that you had rung the bell in order to deceive me in another foolish attempt to escape without returning remittance. So of course I lay in wait for you.

THE HUSBAND. But how did you get around from the front door *(pointing downstage from the counter)* to the back door *(pointing upstage from the counter).*

THE ATTENDANT (AS DOCTOR). I walked.

He reaches out to THE WIFE *for her coat. He helps her off with it. He holds it out to* THE HUSBAND, *who is thinking and distracted. Flatly,* Coat, sir.

THE HUSBAND *takes the coat and hangs it on the clothes tree.*

THE HUSBAND *looks around. Thinking. To himself.* There must be some way we can get out of here without being seen. *He points.* There. The ventilation duct. We could crawl out through that. We could just take off the grill—

THE ATTENDANT (AS DOCTOR). This is a modern symbolic comedy, sir, not a television mystery show. I've taken special care to have the grill over the ventilation duct welded in place. It cannot be removed.

THE HUSBAND. *Pointing.* We'll go out through this window and up the fire escape onto the roof and—

THE ATTENDANT (AS DOCTOR). I have men stationed on the roof, sir.

THE HUSBAND. We could drop down the laundry chute—

THE ATTENDANT (AS DOCTOR). I also have a man stationed in the basement by the laundry hamper, sir. You'd only fall into his hands.

He hands THE HUSBAND *a piece of paper. As* he *speaks,* THE HUSBAND *tears the paper to pieces and throws them away. Yawning.* Excuse me, please, folks, I'm going to turn in now. *Explaining, indicating his watch.* I always take a nap at this time of day. To give my feet a rest. You can't imaging how fatiguing it is to the feet to sit listening to different old people complain about the same old symptoms of disease and about death. *He walks stage left, yawning.*

At the right edge of the stage, downstage of the counter, he halts and turns around. Casually. So you see, sir, there's no use in trying to get away again. The attempt would be futile. Escape is impossible. No one has ever escaped. *He smiles broadly and goes off stage.*

THE HUSBAND *paces to and fro. He considers, his hand at his chin.* If only . . . if only there were no . . . object at all. *Casual, disparaging.* If only that fertile rabbit over there *(indicating* THE WIFE) didn't have to go and have herself an object.

THE WIFE. *Sharply.* Takes two, lover. Last I heard, Mary is the last immaculate conceiver.

THE HUSBAND. I really wish there *wasn't* an object. . . . I don't really think there *is* an object. . . . In fact, I'm *sure* there isn't an object. . . . There is *not* an object. . . . *He sighs deeply. Relieved, brightly.* There now. I feel an awful lot better now that there isn't an object.

THE WIFE. *Flatly, indifferent.* There *is* a baby.

THE HUSBAND, *abruptly clutching his abdomen, grimacing and groaning.* Aaaahhhh.

THE WIFE. Not *that* again. Haven't you been paying attention? Now the baby's over *there. She points at* THE INFANT, on the sofa.

THE HUSBAND *abruptly straightens up and recovers himself. Deliberates.* If only . . . if only . . . I could make the . . . the object . . . . disappear . . . vanish . . get rid of it . . . . dispose of it. . . . How?

THE WIFE. *Flatly.* Commit him to Marcy. Denounce him to the F.B.I. Make him join the army. Send him to Yale.

THE HUSBAND *considers.* Hmm. *He takes off his tie and goes through the motions of strangling himself with it.*

He goes to THE INFANT *and takes him by the arm.* Come here, kid. I want

The Arrival

to show you something. *He draws* THE INFANT *to the downstage
center of the stage.*
THE INFANT. What?
HUSBAND. The view. *He points towards the audience.* Look there, across the
river. See all the factories and warehouses, all the smoke and smog, the
soot, the dirt, the trash, the muck. *In a honeyed tone.* That's *New Jersey.* THE
INFANT *looks towards the audience.* THE HUSBAND *forms the tie into a loop.*
THE WIFE, *speaking as if out of character.* To no one in particular. This is getting
pretty brutal for a comedy, isn't it? *To the audience.* The theme now becomes
one of violence. But we have the American grit to bear with it, don't we?
THE INFANT. You'd better hurry up. I don't know how much longer I can
stand the sight of New Jersey.
    THE HUSBAND *slips the loop of the tie over* THE INFANT's *head.* THE INFANT
ducks out of the loop just before THE HUSBAND *quickly tightens it.* THE INFANT
skips away from THE HUSBAND *and stands facing him.*
THE HUSBAND. Gruffly. You *knew* I was trying to murder you. How? . . .
    Dispassionately, trying to solve the puzzle. You guessed that I made up all that
about New Jersey. You saw the necktie. You put two and two together—
THE INFANT. No, I didn't.
THE HUSBAND. How then?
THE INFANT points at THE HUSBAND's eyes. I saw the murderous gleam in
your eye. He bolts and runs to the right and runs off stage.
    THE HUSBAND *bolts and runs after him, pursuing him closely.*
    There is an interval.
    THE INFANT, *pursued closely by* THE HUSBAND, *runs on stage from the right.*
They run across the stage and off stage.
    There is an interval.
    THE HUSBAND *runs on stage from the left. He runs to the center of the downstage,
downstage from the sofa. He halts and looks around, frowning. He walks toward the right,
looking around, searching, and walks off stage to the right.* THE INFANT *comes on stage
warily from the left, looks around and conceals himself behind the sofa.*
    There is an interval.
    THE HUSBAND *walks on from the right, wearing the tie knotted recklessly and
carrying a pistol. He walks to the center of the downstage, looking around and holding the*

pistol at the ready.

THE WIFE. Where'd you get the pistol? *Answering her own question. Positively.* You bought the pistol a minute ago at Sam's Sporting Goods Store.

THE HUSBAND. *Forceful.* Are you *nuts?* I'm gonna pay   at *Sam's Sporting Goods?* No, *Don's Discount House,* Home of the Good Stuff Cheap.

THE WIFE. *Scornfully.* Cheaper still at Don's Discount House if you'd stolen it.

THE HUSBAND. *As if sorry he hadn't thought of that.* Oh! Yeah. You're right. *Regretful.* That's right. I forgot. It's been a long day.

Where is that sly, sneaky, sniveling little lily-livered midget object? *He steps in front of the sofa, turns around and crouches down.* We'll lie in wait for it here. We'll use this as a blind. It'll come by this way.

THE WIFE. Yeah? How come?

THE HUSBAND. As if it weren't obvious. This is the way to the watering hole.

THE WIFE. "The watering hole" . . .

THE HUSBAND *crouches in front of the sofa and looks upstage right over the back of it. the pistol at the ready.* It'll be by any second.

THE WIFE. *Looking at* THE INFANT *behind the sofa.* Maybe yes, maybe no.

THE HUSBAND. Quiet. . . . Watch.

#

THE INFANT *quickly comes out from behind the sofa. He steps swiftly to the center of the stage and looks at* THE HUSBAND *apprehensively. He clasps his hands to his head in a gesture of bewilderment. He looks anxiously this way and that, as if looking for some way of escape. He rushes confusedly first in one direction and then another. He looks at the door in the back wall, runs to the stairs, quickly mounts them and tries to open the door. As it is locked, he cannot open it. He quickly descends the stairs and runs to the center of the stage and looks around. He looks at the platform. He quickly goes to the stepladder and begins to climb it.* THE DIRECTOR *raps the table with the baton and motions for him to descend the ladder.* THE INFANT *descends the ladder and stands looking at* THE DIRECTOR. THE DIRECTOR *motions him away from the ladder.* THE INFANT *backs away from it.*

THE INFANT *clears his throat.* To THE DIRECTOR. Uh . . . Mister—

THE DIRECTOR *cuts* THE INFANT *short, rapping on the table, and motions him to kneel.* THE INFANT *kneels.* THE DIRECTOR *motions him to stand up and* THE INFANT *stands up.*

THE INFANT. Mister Soldier . . .

THE DIRECTOR *frowns and shakes his head. He points at insignia on his jacket and cap.*

THE INFANT. Sergeant—

THE DIRECTOR *instantly slams the baton against the arm of the chair with great force and leaps to his feet. He grimaces in outrage, furiously clasps and unclasps his hands and points again at the insignia on his shoulders and hat and points in an upward direction with the baton.*

THE INFANT. Sir—

THE DIRECTOR *raps the table with the baton and shakes his head.*

THE INFANT. Mein Herr . . . . THE DIRECTOR *shakes his head after* THE INFANT *says each title, except the last one.* Mynheer . . . Mirza . . . Effendi. THE DIRECTOR, *shaking his head, again points up with the stick.* Captain . . . Colonel . . . General . .. Chairman of the Board . . . Your Lordship . . . Your Grace . . . Your Highness . .. Your Majesty . . . Sire . . . Great Leader of the Revolution . . . Our Master . . . Lord of Hosts . .. THE DIRECTOR *smiles, folds his arms on his chest and sits down.* May I come up there, mister?

THE DIRECTOR shakes his head.

THE INFANT. I would like very much to, if I may.

THE DIRECTOR again shakes his head.

THE INFANT. Please let me, mister.

THE DIRECTOR *shakes his head.*

THE INFANT. *Pointing at* THE HUSBAND. Do you see that big dummy over there, mister?

THE DIRECTOR *nods.*

THE INFANT. He's hunting me down. He has a gun. If he finds me he'll shoot me. I must find a safe place to hide.

THE DIRECTOR *shrugs his shoulders indifferently and wears an indifferent expression.*

THE INFANT. I *would* be safe from him up there, wouldn't I, mister?

THE DIRECTOR *nods.*

THE INFANT. There's room for me up there, isn't there, mister?
  THE DIRECTOR *nods.*
THE INFANT. Then you'll let me climb up there, won't you, mister?
  THE DIRECTOR *shakes his head.*
THE INFANT. You're being awfully cruel, aren't you, mister.
  THE DIRECTOR *nods.*
THE INFANT. Anxiously. But, mister, he'll shoot me!
  THE DIRECTOR *wears a blank expression.*
THE INFANT. He *will* shoot me, won't he, mister?
  THE DIRECTOR *continues to wear a blank expression.*
THE INFANT. You know if he will.
  THE DIRECTOR *nods.*
THE INFANT. But you won't tell.
  THE DIRECTOR *shakes his head.*
THE INFANT. Then you'll tell me where there's a safe place to hide down
  here, won't you, mister?
  THE DIRECTOR *again wears a blank expression.*
THE INFANT. You don't know where there's a safe place to hide down here.
  THE DIRECTOR *raps the table with the baton and scowls at* THE INFANT.
THE INFANT. You *do* know.
  THE DIRECTOR *nods.*
THE INFANT. But you won't tell.
  THE DIRECTOR *shakes his head.*
THE INFANT *looks away from* THE DIRECTOR. *To himself.* Isn't there somebody
  who'll help me find a safe place to hide?
  THE DIRECTOR *has heard this and shakes his head.*
THE INFANT. *Looking at* THE DIRECTOR. God, he *is* a bastard. (*This line is read
so that it can be understood both as, "God! he is a bastard," and, "God: He is a
bastard."*)

THE WIFE. *To The Husband looking upstage right.* I don't like to ever dispel any
  of your cherished illusions but the fact is that the person you're on the
  look-out for is standing right behind you.

THE HUSBAND *continues to look over the back of the sofa.* Quiet! Do you want to scare it away? . . . Where is it? Do you see it? I don't see it yet. Is that it over there? . . . No, that's not it. . . . *He pauses. Calmly.* You did say that it's standing right behind me, didn't you?

THE WIFE. Yes I did.

THE HUSBAND. Slippery little devil, isn't it? *He slowly stands up and faces* THE INFANT. *He starts and points at* THE INFANT. There it is! What did I tell you!

THE INFANT *bolts and runs off stage right.* THE HUSBAND *runs off after him firing the pistol. The pistol is fired offstage.*

There is an interval of about ten seconds.

THE INFANT *runs on from the right. He runs to the sofa and conceals himself behind it.*

THE HUSBAND *runs on stage from the right, He holds the pistol at the ready. He looks around. Suddenly points at the chair.*

THE HUSBAND. Hah! There it is! *He fires the pistol towards the chair.* THE INFANT's *head momentarily appears above the back of the sofa. Pointing to where* THE INFANT's *head appeared.* Hah! There it is! *He fires the pistol towards the sofa, holding the pistol behind his back in the manner of a trick-shooter. Proudly, to* THE WIFE. Buffalo Bill's grandson taught me that trick.

THE WIFE. I didn't know there were any wild buffalo left to shoot.

THE HUSBAND. He doesn't shoot wild buffalo.

THE WIFE. What does he shoot?

THE HUSBAND. He shoots wild drunks: he's a bartender. . . . Got it. Right between the eyes.

THE WIFE. *Flatly.* No, you missed it.

THE HUSBAND. What! Missed! I did! Damn! *He paces to and from, scowling. He halts. Solemn.* Yes. I missed. Do you know what that means?

THE WIFE. It means you're a rotten shot, I suppose.

THE HUSBAND. *Solemn.* It means that I will have to . . . *go* . . . *in* . . . . *after* . . *it.*

THE WIFE. In where?

THE HUSBAND. *Solemn.* Why, into the elephant grass, of course. . . . *With an English accent.* Sticky business, this. Nasty. See absolutely nothing in the grass. Beast jumps you. On you in half a mo. Then no chance, of course:

game's up. Got to be done, though. No help for it. Best screw up one's pluck and make the best of a bad job. Good show, that's what's wanted. Can't funk it. Wouldn't do. One's standards, you know. A chap's honor, duty, loyalty and all that. For the sake of a bloke's country, family, college fraternity and civic-improvement association.

THE WIFE. *With the vehemence that might be expected if* THE HUSBAND *had committed some abhorrent sexual act.* Oh my *God!* Not *that again!* Gotta be he's been *dabbling in English literature again!*

THE HUSBAND *gets down on his hands and knees and begins to crawl counterclockwise around the sofa.* THE INFANT *also crawls counterclockwise around the sofa, keeping the sofa between him and* THE HUSBAND, *as if to conceal himself from* THE HUSBAND behind it.

THE HUSBAND. The Great White Hunter, the greatest of all the white hunters, proceeds with extreme caution through the nearly impenetrable jungle underbrush. He does not know how far away or near danger lurks in the dark foliage. The Wild Jungle Beast may be hidden only a few short feet from him, ready to pounce upon him and tear him to ribbons.

THE WIFE. *Gravely.* "The Great White Hunter"? *Tapping her head with her finger.* This may be more despicable than I thought.

THE HUSBAND *abruptly halts and listens with an alarmed expression.* What's that I hear? Thump. Thump. Thump. What is it? *Excited.* It's getting louder! Where's it coming from! *To* THE WIFE. Don't you hear it! *He looks around with greater and greater alarm.* It's getting louder and louder and faster and faster! Thumpity-thumpity-thumpity. What is it!

THE WIFE. That's your heart you hear, you booby.

THE HUSBAND *sighs with relief.* Whew! Thank heavens! That was scary.!

THE INFANT *crawls up onto the seat of the sofa.* THE HUSBAND *crawls around the sofa keeping his nose close to the floor like a trailing dog. He halts in front of the sofa.*

THE HUSBAND. The Great White Hunter sniffs the air. *He lifts his head from the floor and, looking away from* THE INFANT, *sniffs loudly.* He has a sense of smell as keen as a bloodhound's. He detects a faint odor of the beast. Now he knows that the beast is not far away—maybe even quite near.

THE WIFE. For once you're right. [nope]

THE HUSBAND. *Looking closely at the floor.* Ahah! Fresh tracks! We'll catch it if we hurry. *He begins to crawl swiftly around the sofa.*

When THE HUSBAND *disappears behind the sofa,* THE INFANT *runs to the chair and conceals himself behind it.*

THE HUSBAND *crawls in front of the sofa. He sniffs loudly. He frowns.* That's funny. The faint odor I detect now is fainter than before. *He quickly gets to his feet. Angrily to* THE WIFE. You let it get away!

THE WIFE. *Flatly.* You're in charge here. You're THE HUSBAND. You're the man. You're the one with the gun.

THE HUSBAND *looks around. He gets down on his hands and knees and looks under the sofa..*

THE WIFE. *Sarcastic.* Maybe he's under the rug.

THE HUSBAND. *Serious.* What rug? Where? There isn't any rug.

THE WIFE. *Scornful.* I was being sarcastic.

THE HUSBAND. *Exasperated.* I *know* you were being sarcastic. You're *always* being sarcastic. . . *Serious.* But where did you say the rug is? . . . He looks about and considers. What *is* that immature person now?

Incidentally, I was taught to shoot by the grandson of Buffalo Bill.

THE WIFE. *Playing along.* Umm-hmm. Shooting wild buffalo . . . .

THE HUSBAND. What! Wild buffalo? How can he shoot wild buffalo? There are no wild buffalo left to shoot.

THE WIFE. What does he shoot?

THE HUSBAND. Wild drunks. He's a bartender.

THE WIFE. Oh my God. Now we're forced to endure the English.

The Husband *walks around, searching, the pistol at the ready. He walks counterclockwise around the sofa.* THE INFANT meanwhile walks backwards counter-clockwise around the sofa, keeping it between him and THE HUSBAND. *The Infant backs into* THE HUSBAND. THE HUSBAND *is startled. He spins around and grabs* THE INFANT *by the neck. He points the pistol at his head. Ahah!* Got you! Stick 'em up! Quick! THE INFANT *raises his hands.* Don't move! I've got you cornered. *He frowns. Puzzled.* "Cornered"? . . . That doesn't sound quite right. How does that go? *Frowning.* "I've got you *'cornered'?*" . . . His face suddenly lights up. *"Covered"!* That's it! . . . *To* THE INFANT, *menacingly.* Don't move. I've got you *covered. Very pleased with himself.* Hah! I did it! I caught it!

He chuckles. To THE WIFE. Did you see me catch it? Did you?

THE WIFE. I saw him bump into you when you weren't looking, if that's what you mean.

THE HUSBAND. I'm some hunter, huh?

THE WIFE. *Sarcastically.* Oh yes. Certainly, certainly. Quite a hunter.

THE HUSBAND. I never brag and I never tell a lie so I'll just tell you the plain honest truth: I'm a hero.

THE WIFE. Oh yes. Yes indeed. You're a great hero. Yes indeed.

THE HUSBAND. *In a masterful tone to* THE INFANT. Well, now, I bet you're going to say that really you're tired of running from us, aren't you? I bet you're going to say that really you're kind of glad we've fiinally caught up with you, aren't you?

THE INFANT. No.

THE HUSBAND. You're not! Is that the kind of answer somebody is supposed to give at a time like this? Don't you go to the movies? Look. You'd better watch what you say to me. Or I'll do something to your worse than blowing your brains out. I'll . .. I'll wrap you in waxpaper and throw you in the trash can. . . . I'll . . flush you down the hopper. . . . I'll cut your guts out and throw them to the wolves. . . I'll cut your heart out and pickle it in vinegar. *That's* what I'll do to you.

THE INFANT. *Calmly.* It's possible. I believe such things have been reported in the popular press.

THE HUSBAND. However, since I've already bought a pistol and since it's only sound business practice for me to make good use of what I've already bought . . . Well?

THE INFANT. Well what?

THE HUSBAND. Have you got any last words?

THE INFANT. *Looking around.* Why? Is someone recording this? . . . Well, let me see . . . I don't *think* I'm going to miss you terribly. No, if it's all the same to you, you can take you your time showing up for the obligatory heavenly reunion. . . . He shrugs his shoulders. Oh well. Maybe better luck next time around.

THE HUSBAND *suddenly lets the hand holding the pistol drop and assumes a thoughtful expressioin.* Wait. I've got an idea. It would save the price of a bullet. He puts the pistol in his pocket. The Great White Hunter has no gun. He battles the Wild Jungle Beast with only his bare hands. *Casually, to* THE WIFE. It's only fair to give it a sporting chance, don't you think, dearie? THE INFANT *suddenly runs to the end table.* THE HUSBAND *runs after him.* THE INFANT, *on the run, take the bell [how did this bell get there?] from the end table and begins to ring it. He runs clockwise around the chair.* THE HUSBAND *runs after him around the chair and catches him at center stage.*

THE HUSBAND. Got you! The great jungle battle is on. . . . The Wild Jungle Beast attacks. *He takes* THE INFANT *by the throat.* THE INFANT *rings the bell as* THE HUSBAND *speaks.* The Great White Hunter skillfully fends off the blow. *He throttles* THE INFANT. The Great White Hunter counterattacks. He takes the Wild Jungle Beast by the throat. He holds the Wild Jungle Beast in his super-strong, steely grip. They wrestle to the ground locked in titanic, mortal combat. *He forces* THE INFANT to *the floor.* THE INFANT *lies supine. He sits astride* THE INFANT, *his hands·around* THE INFANT's *throat.* THE INFANT *continues to ring the bell.* The Wild Jungle Beast tries to break away from the Great White Hunter's deadly grasp. But the Wild Jungle Beast cannot break away, powerful as the Wild Jungle Beast is. It slashes wildly at the Great White Hunter with its long, razor-sharp claws. The Great White Hunter adeptly avoids them, moving as fast as lightning. The Great Whnite Hunter squeezes tighter and tighter on the Wild Jungle Beast's throat. He slowly chokes the life out of the Wild Jungle Beast. THE INFANT *rings the bell more and more feebly.* The Wild Jungle Beast dies.

THE INFANT *rings the bell very feebly.*

#

THE ATTENDANT (AS DOCTOR) *walks on very slowly from the right, yawning. Annoyed.* All right. All right. I'm coming. I'm coming. Where's the fire? *He sees* THE HUSBAND *and* THE INFANT. *He is startled and rushes to them. He pulls at* THE HUSBAND. Sir! Get up! Get off that child, sir! You can't do that! You know the rules, sir! It is absolutely forbidden to manhandle the featured items! . . . Don't force me to resort to the pleasant step of breaking your neck, sir! . . . Get up now, sir! This is outrageous! Intolerable! Shocking! Rule-breaking! I've never heard of such a thing! . . . Wouldn't cha know?—something like this is always happening! . . . I'm not surprised at you, sir. I certainly expected something like this from you! . . . Get up now! Get up, sir! THE HUSBAND *stands up and* THE ATTENDANT (AS DOCTOR) *pulls him away from* THE INFANT. *In an exaggeratedly injured tone.* After all I've done for you, sir—is this any way to behave towards me!

He goes to THE INFANT, *who is lying on the floor, kneels and examines him.* Good! It's *alive! He looks at* THE INFANT *more closely.* And well! . . . *Flatly.* The neck's a little worried, is all.

He pulls THE INFANT *abruptly to his feet.* It's a good thing I got here when I did. Luckily I rushed here with no more than average procrastination.

He steps to THE HUSBAND. Gravely. Now tell me, sir, I know you weren't trying to do it harm, but what exactly were you doing with your hands around its neck?

THE HUSBAND. Do I have to make up a story?

THE ATTENDANT (AS DOCTOR). I think it would be very nice if you did, sir.

THE HUSBAND. Well, then . . . It was choking. There was a fish-bone caught in its throat. I was just trying to work it loose.

THE ATTENDANT (AS DOCTOR). Hmm. A very unlikely story, sir.

THE HUSBAND. *I* thought so.

THE ATTENDANT (AS DOCTOR). And of course I believe it. . . . And I didn't hear shots a little while ago, either.

THE HUSBAND. Right.

THE ATTENDANT (AS DOCTOR). And you don't have a pistol in that pocket. He points at the pocket.

THE HUSBAND. Right..

THE ATTENDANT (AS DOCTOR). *As he speaks he quickly steps behind* THE HUSBAND. THE HUSBAND *pays no attention to him. He takes the pistol from* THE HUSBAND's *jacket pocket. He puts it in his own jacket pocket. He steps back in front of* THE HUSBAND. All the same, sir, perhaps it would interest you to know—purely as a point of commercial information— that there is a certain party who just happens to be standing face-to-face with me at this very moment and who has very definitely entered into a binding contract and who will very definitely pay through the nose before he leaves these premises and that that certain party is very definitely very sadly mistaken if he believes that he will be permitted to liquidate the contracted-for goods under the assumption that such damage by him to the contracted-for goods constitutes good and sufficient grounds for release from his fore-assumed obligation to fork over the cash.

THE HUSBAND *looks puzzled. He frowns and scratches his head.* That's *philosophy,* isn't it?

THE ATTENDANT (AS DOCTOR) *hands* THE HUSBAND a piece of paper. *Yawning.* Pay, sir.

THE HUSBAND *places the paper on his head as if it were a hat. He frowns and tosses the paper away.*

THE ATTENDANT (AS DOCTOR) *grasps the lapels of* THE HUSBAND's *jacket. Flatly.* Oh no. I'll make you pay, sir.

THE HUSBAND *breaks away from* THE ATTENDANT (AS DOCTOR)'s *grasp with a flourish. He backs away from him and stands facing him. His hand is poised over the pocket from which* THE ATTENDANT (AS DOCTOR) *has taken the pistol.* No you're not. Don't try anything. Stand right were you are. I've got you covered— (*he quickly corrects himself*)—cornered—(*he quickly corrects himself again*)—covered. Don't move or I'll—

THE ATTENDANT (AS DOCTOR). *Disdainfully.* You can't intimidate me with mere threats of violence, sir. *Thinks for a second about what he has just said. Corrects himself.* —threats of mere violence, sir. *Short pause.* Godammit, now he's got *me* doing it.

THE HUSBAND. What would you say if I told you it just so happens that I bought a pistol a minute ago at Don's Discount House and that it's right here in my pocket? *He indicates the pocket.*

THE ATTENDANT (AS DOCTOR) *smiles knowingly. He makes a show of thinking. Shrewdly.* I rather doubt that, sir

THE HUSBAND. What if I told you I bought *two* pistols a minute ago at Don's Discount House? THE DIRECTOR *wraps on the umpire's chair with his baton.*

The Arrival

THE ATTENDANT (AS DOCTOR) *is startled. Apprehensive.* What! *Two* pistols!
   Two!
THE HUSBAND. *Casual.* No. I was just kidding. I only bought one. Why
   should I buy *two* pistols a minute ago at Don's Discount House?
THE ATTENDANT (AS DOCTOR) *takes a step towards* THE HUSBAND. Pay, sir.
THE HUSBAND. If you take another step, I'll shoot.
THE ATTENDANT (AS DOCTOR). *Out of character. Loudly addressing the audience.*
   God this is exciting, isn't it, folks?
[THE DIRECTOR's actions in connection with the above dialogue]
   He takes another step towards THE HUSBAND.
THE HUSBAND *reaches into his pocket for the pistol. He assumes a shocked expression.*
   My pistol! My pistol! Where'd it go?
THE ATTENDANT (AS DOCTOR) *smiles. He takes the pistol from his pocket and
   points it at* THE HUSBAND. Here's your pistol, sir. . . . *In an amiable tone.*
   Pay, sir.
THE HUSBAND. I don't have any money.
THE ATTENDANT (AS DOCTOR). Then you lie even under the threat of death?
THE HUSBAND. No.
THE ATTENDANT (AS DOCTOR). So you *are* lying?
THE HUSBAND. No
THE ATTENDANT (AS DOCTOR). *Amiable.* Good for you, sir. I see you
   understand that that's one of the very best times to lie. . . . Pay, sir.
   Abruptly THE HUSBAND is *dejected. He paces to and fro. He makes dejected*
*gestures and shakes his bowed head. He halts. He puts his hands to his chest on the left
side, over his wallet. He shakes his head sadly and glares at* THE ATTENDANT (AS
DOCTOR). *He paces to and fro. He halts. He takes his handkerchief from his pocket and
wipes his eyes. He covers his face with his handkerchief.*
THE ATTENDANT (AS DOCTOR) *puts his arm around* THE HUSBAND's
   shoulders. *Soothingly.* Come on, sir. Buck up. Don't cry, sir. With his free
   hand he reaches inside THE HUSBAND's jacket for his wallet. THE
   HUSBAND pushes his hand away. *Casually.* Just relax. I'll give you your
   wallet back just as soon as I've taken the money out of it. *As he speaks he
   continues to reach for* THE HUSBAND's *wallet.* THE HUSBAND *continues to push*

his hand away. Soothing. Life is a hard road to travel, sir. We can't all be rich like me. Everybody can't be a winner. Somebody has to be the prize booby like you. *Abruptly cheerful.* Which reminds me: we have a booby prize for you as a sincere token of our appreciation the all the kale we're conning out of you. It's an absolutely free going-away gift. Excuse me, sir, I'll get it for you.

 He begins to walk towards stage left. He halts. Speaking as if out of character. Addressing the audience. Looking at his watch. Incidentally, folks, I see the hour is getting on, so if any of you feel you ought to go along home now to relieve babysitter, please feel entirely free to do so. We up here *(he indicates the stage)* won't be in the least offended. Just be as quiet as possible on your way out, please. The box office is closed so there's no question of demanding your money back. *He smiles and goes off stage left.*

#

THE HUSBAND *paces to and fro. He deliberates, holding his hand to his chin.* What to do now . . . . *He paces. He halts and holds up his finger.* What I'm going to do now is . . . *poison* it. *He paces and halts. He holds up his finger.*
THE WIFE. And then take it to the Customer Service Desk.
 THE HUSBAND *nods.*
THE HUSBAND *paces to and fro. He halts and holds up his finger.* And return it. *He nods. He paces, He halts and holds up his finger.*
THE WIFE. For a refund in full.
 THE HUSBAND *nods.*
THE HUSBAND *takes a very large lollipop wrapped in paper from his pocket. He walks to* THE INFANT. *To* THE INFANT. Still hungry? Here. *He hands the lollipop to* THE INFANT. Umm. Good. Yum-yum-yum. Lemon arsenic. *He steps to center stage.*
 THE ATTENDANT (AS DOCTOR) *comes on from the stage left. He carries a basket of fruit. He eats a banana.*
THE HUSBAND. *With polite gratitude.* Oh, isn't that nice. That's real considerate

107

of you. Thank you very much.

THE ATTENDANT (AS DOCTOR). *Speaking with his mouth full of the banana.* That'll be sixty-seven dollars extra.

THE HUSBAND. Fifty dollars! But you said it was an absolutely free going-away gift!

THE ATTENDANT (AS DOCTOR). *His mouth still full of banana.* Carrying charge, sir. THE HUSBAND *looks at him quizzically.* You saw me carry it in here, didn't you? . . . *He takes an apple from the basket and puts it in the right-hand pocket of his jacket.*

THE HUSBAND. Hey! What are you doing! Put that apple back!

THE ATTENDANT (AS DOCTOR). You're mistaken, sir. I didn't take any apple.

THE HUSBAND *takes the cores of eaten apples, grape vine stems from which the grapes have been removed, and orange peels from the basket.* Hey! What's the idea!

THE ATTENDANT (AS DOCTOR). Caveat emptor, sir.

THE HUSBAND *points to the right-hand pocket of* THE ATTENDANT (AS DOCTOR)'s *jacket.* Give me the apple you just took!

THE ATTENDANT (AS DOCTOR). That's no apple in my pocket. That's a baseball.

THE HUSBAND. A *baseball!* Are you crazy! What would you be doing with a *baseball* in your pocket!

THE ATTENDANT (AS DOCTOR) *shrugs his shoulders and hesitates.* It's a baseball.

THE HUSBAND. Hah! Show it to me! Take it out of your pocket!

THE ATTENDANT (AS DOCTOR). Certainly, sir. *He puts his hand in the pocket.*

THE HUSBAND *grabs his arm. Calmly, confidently.* Wait. Let's make sure we've got this straight. *I* say you took an apple from that basket and put it in your pocket and *you* say it's a baseball in your pocket. Is that right?

THE ATTENDANT (AS DOCTOR). You haven't been listening?

THE HUSBAND. *Confident.* All right. We'll see who's lying. Go on take it out.

THE ATTENDANT (AS DOCTOR) *pauses with his hand in the pocket.* You suspect a trick, perhaps? . . . Somehow I have the feeling you don't entirely trust me.

THE HUSBAND. Take it out. Go on.

THE ATTENDANT (AS DOCTOR) *again pauses. Loudly to the audience.* The suspense is killing, isn't it? A fitting climax to an evening of high excitement, don't you think?

THE HUSBAND. *Impatiently.* Take it out, damn you!

THE ATTENDANT (AS DOCTOR) *takes the apple from his pocket. He frowns and looks puzzled.*

THE HUSBAND. Ahah! An apple! Isn't it an apple!

THE ATTENDANT (AS DOCTOR). *Frowning, looking closely at the apple.* Evidently. . . . Would you like to see some other of my magic tricks?

THE HUSBAND. *Scoffing.* As if you carried a *baseball* around with you!

THE ATTENDANT (AS DOCTOR) *takes a baseball from the left-hand pocket of his jacket.* Ah. There it is. . . . I guess I got the pockets mixed up. Explaining. Some of us boys toss a few back and forth during lunch hour, sir. *He puts the baseball back in his pocket and begins to eat the apple. Pointing the pistol at* THE HUSBAND. *Chewing the apple. Amiable.* Pay, sir.

THE HUSBAND. I'm not going to pay for that fruit basket! You ate the fruit in that basket yourself!

THE ATTENDANT (AS DOCTOR). No, sir. . . . Yes, sir. *He shrugs his shoulders indifferently. He hands* THE HUSBAND *a piece of paper.* Chewing the apple. Pay, sir.

THE HUSBAND *crumples the paper into a ball and punts it away as if it were a football.*

THE HUSBAND. I'm not paying for that, either! *He points at* THE INFANT. I don't have to. I'm not paying for a dead horse.

THE ATTENDANT (AS DOCTOR). What do you mean?

THE HUSBAND. It's dead.

THE ATTENDANT (AS DOCTOR). Dead!

THE HUSBAND. That's right. Poisoned.

THE ATTENDANT (AS DOCTOR). I told you, sir, that you're very sadly mistaken if you think you can avoid payment by liquidating the purchased item.

THE HUSBAND. I didn't liquidate it. It was an accident. It was playing with a lollipop. It didn't know the lollipop was loaded—*(he pauses)*—with poison.

THE ATTENDANT (AS DOCTOR) *goes to the sofa.* THE INFANT *sits without moving.* THE ATTENDANT (AS DOCTOR) *bends over him and examines him closely.*

THE ATTENDANT (AS DOCTOR). There's nothing wrong with this.

THE HUSBAND *starts violently* . *What!* . . . *Abruptly suspicious.* Oh no. Oh no. You're not going to get away with that. It's dead and I'm not going to pay for it.

THE ATTENDANT (AS DOCTOR). It's *not* dead, sir. It's very much alive. Come here and see.

THE HUSBAND. Lying never did anybody any good.

THE INFANT. He's right. I'm quite all right.

THE HUSBAND *starts. What! He rushes to the sofa.*

THE ATTENDANT (AS DOCTOR). You see, sir. It's not in the least dead. Not even a little bit.

THE HUSBAND. But that's impossible.

THE ATTENDANT (AS DOCTOR). In fact, sir, it appears to be in top-notch A-number-one condition.

THE HUSBAND. Impossible! . . . It's alive! . . . God damn! . . . Why, it hasn't even unwrapped the lollipop! *He snatches the lollipop from* THE INFANT's *hand. He tears off the wrapping and thrusts it at* THE INFANT. *Here! Eat it! Lick away!*

THE INFANT *does not take the lollipop.* I don't really want it.

THE HUSBAND. Why not!

THE INFANT. You say it's lemon?

THE HUSBAND. Yes, lemon arsenic.

THE INFANT. I'd rather have lime.

THE HUSBAND. Ah! *He throws the lollipop onto the stage, He claps his hands to his head in despair. He paces to and fro. He holds his hands to his forehead and groans. He halts. He throws out his arms and exclaims in despair. He shakes his fists and hits his head with them. He grimaces and groans.*

THE WIFE. You must not be living right.

THE ATTENDANT (AS DOCTOR) *bites into the apple. He hands* THE HUSBAND *a piece of paper. Chewing.* Pay, sir.

THE HUSBAND *tears the piece of paper to pieces and puts them in his pocket.*

THE HUSBAND. I don't have that much money. *He turns away from* THE ATTENDANT (AS DOCTOR), *takes some money from his wallet, turns and hands it to* THE ATTENDANT (AS DOCTOR). That's all the money I have.

The ArrivalTHE ATTENDANT (AS DOCTOR). *Counts the money.* This is only half the amount due, sir.

THE HUSBAND. That's all the money I have. THE ATTENDANT (AS DOCTOR) *glares at him. Abruptly his tone turns frank and earnest.* Honest. That's all the money I have.

THE ATTENDANT (AS DOCTOR). *Agreeably.* That's all right, sir. This amount will be sufficient.

THE HUSBAND. *Puzzled. What!* "Sufficient"? . . . You give up pretty easy, don't you? Aren't you going to try to squeeze me some more?

THE ATTENDANT (AS DOCTOR). I am satisfied for now to receive this amount, sir. . . . Now, if you'd like, you can give me back that false bill I gave you.

THE HUSBAND. False bill?

THE ATTENDANT (AS DOCTOR). Yes. The bill I gave you is a false bill. I wrote it purely for bargaining purposes. THE HUSBAND *takes the pieces of paper from his pocket. He holds them out to* THE ATTENDANT (AS DOCTOR). THE ATTENDANT (AS DOCTOR) *ignores him.* THE HUSBAND *drops the pieces of paper on the floor.* THE ATTENDANT (AS DOCTOR) *takes a sheet of paper from his pocket.* Here is the true bill. It is for an amount one quarter as large. . . . Oh, I wouldn't feel too lucky if I were you, sir. I'm still charging you ten times what is fair and reasonable. . . . So you see—or you would see if you were as clever at figures as I am—that you have paid me twice what is necessary.

THE HUSBAND. Then give me half of it back.

THE ATTENDANT (AS DOCTOR). *Amiably.* Oh no, sir. I couldn't do that. That's cabbage.

THE HUSBAND. Cabbage?

THE ATTENDANT (AS DOCTOR). A perquisite.

THE HUSBAND. Perquisite?

THE ATTENDANT (AS DOCTOR). A tip. For which, of course, I thank you very heartily. *He smiles and bows.*

THE HUSBAND. *Stern.* Give it back.

THE ATTENDANT (AS DOCTOR). Impossible, sir. . . . *He looks at the pistol.* Oh,

I'm sorry. I guess this is yours. *He holds out the pistol to* THE HUSBAND.
THE HUSBAND *takes the pistol. He wears a puzzled expression. He looks at the pistol
for a moment and then points it at* THE ATTENDANT (AS DOCTOR). Grimly.
Give me back the money I gave you. All of it.
THE ATTENDANT (AS DOCTOR). Oh no, sir.
THE HUSBAND. This is your last chance. Give it back.
THE ATTENDANT (AS DOCTOR). Oh no, sir.
THE HUSBAND *fires the pistol at* THE ATTENDANT (AS DOCTOR). THE
ATTENDANT (AS DOCTOR) *stands without moving, smiling.*
THE WIFE. To THE HUSBAND. You missed again.
THE ATTENDANT (AS DOCTOR). *To* THE WIFE. No, ma'am. I took the
sensible precaution just now of substituting blanks for the bullets that
were in your husband's weapon. *To* THE HUSBAND. You see: I get ideas
myself from watching B movies.

THE HUSBAND *paces to and fro. He gestures with greater and greater force.. Two or*

three times he halts, glares at THE ATTENDANT (AS DOCTOR) *and continues to
pace and gesture. He halts and looks at* THE ATTENDANT (AS DOCTOR) *angrily.
Shouting with great vehemence.* This is outrageous! I'm not going to stand for
this! You think I don't know what you're trying to get away with! I know
what you're trying to get away with! *He paces to and fro, turning to shout at*
THE ATTENDANT (AS DOCTOR). I'm not so dumb, you know! I'm not
blind, you know! I can see what's going on right in front of my eyes! I see
what you're trying to get away with! You think you're so smart! Well,
you're not so smart! You're trying to *overcharge* me! *That's* what you're
trying to get away with! Don't deny that's what you're trying to get away
with! I saw you overcharge me! I saw where you put my money! You put
my money in your *pocket. That's* where you put my money. *He points at the
pocket.* Ever since I got here you've been trying to overcharge me! Why,
you don't even care about me! All you care about is my money and how

112

to overcharge me! Well, you can't get away with overcharging me! You can't do that! It's against the law! It's not *fair*. I have my civil rights, you know! I know what my civil rights are! You think you can get away with anything you want to! Well, you can't, you know. Who do you think you are, anyway! You're no better than me, you know! This is a *popular democracy!* Nobody's any better than anybody else in a popular democracy! You think you can get away with overcharging me but I'm not going to *let* you get away with overcharging me! You're going to give me my money back! I'm going to *take* my money back! I'm going to take my money right out of your pocket! *He points at the pocket.* I'm going to put my hand right into that pocket where you put my money and I'm going to take my money right out of it! And you better not try to stop me, either! Because if you try to stop me I'll knock you down! If you try to stop me, I'll break your arm. If you try to stop me, I'll knock your front tooth out! I'm going to take my money right out of your pocket right now! And don't try to stop me! *He stands facing* THE ATTENDANT (AS DOCTOR). *He walks towards* THE ATTENDANT (AS DOCTOR).

THE ATTENDANT (AS DOCTOR) *stands up. He crosses his arms on his chest, He stands stock still and glares at* THE HUSBAND. THE HUSBAND *halts before him and looks up into his face. There is a long pause as they glare at each other.*

THE HUSBAND *takes a backward step, clears his throat and turns towards* THE WIFE. *To* THE WIFE *in a low, defeated voice.* Come on. Let's go.

There is a pause.

He suddenly starts and rushes at THE ATTENDANT (AS DOCTOR) *and seizes the lapels of* THE ATTENDANT (AS DOCTOR)'s *jacket. Shouting in a rage.* Give me back my apple! Give me back my booby prize! Give me back my cabbage.

THE ATTENDANT (AS DOCTOR). *Calmly.* No, sir.

They grapple and scuffle. They wrestle to the floor and roll around, grunting and groaning. THE ATTENDANT (AS DOCTOR) *pins* THE HUSBAND *on his back. He sits astride him and throttles him.* THE HUSBAND *gasps and chokes loudly.*

#

THE DIRECTOR *stands up. He climbs down the umpire's chair and walks to* THE HUSBAND *and* THE ATTENDANT (AS DOCTOR). *He goes through the motion of striking* THE ATTENDANT (AS DOCTOR) *over the head with the baton.* THE ATTENDANT (AS DOCTOR) *rolls off of* THE HUSBAND *onto his back and lies still, as if he has been knocked unconscious.* THE HUSBAND *gets to his feet and dusts off his clothes.*

THE DIRECTOR *walks towards the umpire's chair.* THE HUSBAND *catches him by the shoulder and turns him around.*

THE HUSBAND. *Speaking as if out of character.* Look. You can't just come down from that chair up there and knock this guy on the noggin like that. It just doesn't make any sense. You can't just come down on the stage like that out of the blue and save me, like you was some kind of a . . . some kind of a *god,* you know, or something like that. It just ain't realistic . . . it ain't naturalistic, you understand?

Look. This is the way I see it: the way you got it now you supposedly come down here and rescue this here hero character. All right, at least this *slob*—indicating THE ATTENDANT (AS DOCTOR)—doesn't kill him. But you got it so this *jerk*—(he again indicates THE ATTENDANT (AS DOCTOR))—robs him blind. And he doesn't get any of his money back when he tries to get it back. That's no good. He's short and he's got a family to support. What kind of a finish is that. The audience won't like it. It's unjust.

Here's what you do: you write is so I punch this *creep*—(he indicates THE ATTENDANT (AS DOCTOR))—out. I knock him in the kisser once and he's out, see? And then I take all that money away from him that I gave him. Get it? Why not? . . . All right, I know he's bigger than me. But I could knock that crummy actor off in two seconds anyway, believe me. I'd sure like to, too. . . . Whataya say? Huh? How about it? Huh?

THE DIRECTOR *dismisses him with a shake of his head and a disdainful grimace. He walks to the umpire's chair.*

THE HUSBAND *bends over* THE ATTENDANT (AS DOCTOR), *who continues to lie still. He takes the money from his pocket.*

THE DIRECTOR *raps the baton against the umpire's chair. He motions for* THE
HUSBAND *to return the money to* THE ATTENDANT (AS DOCTOR)s *pocket.*

THE HUSBAND *reluctantly returns the money. Angrily.* Damn it! The scales they're
paying me they ought to let me filch something from this bum! *He kicks*
THE ATTENDANT (AS DOCTOR). THE ATTENDANT (AS DOCTOR) *abruptly
abandons the pretense that he has been knocked unconscious. He angrily seizes a leg of*
THE HUSBAND's *trousers.* THE HUSBAND *pulls out of* THE ATTENDANT (AS
DOCTOR)*'s grasp. Suddenly* THE ATTENDANT (AS DOCTOR) *lies still again,
resuming the pretense that he has been knocked unconscious.*

THE DIRECTOR *climbs the ladder of the umpire's chair and sits down.*

#

THE ATTENDANT (AS DOCTOR), *out of character, suddenly jumps to his feet, and
addresses the audience.* Just a reminder, folks. Before you leave the theater,
please be sure to fill out the survey. The forms will be found in the lobby
on your way out on the table with the tall pile of surpluss *Playbills.* Please
do hesitate to be utterly frank in your opinions about tonight's
presentation. One form will be drawn from those giving us an overall
rating of a perfect ten and also enclosing the stated minimum voluntary
donation. The lucky winner will be awarded a guaranteed winning ticket
in the Wyoming state lottery.

Thank you. Enjoy the rest of the show.

He lies back down on the floor, resuming his role.

There is an interval.

#

THE ATTENDANT (AS DOCTOR) *stirs. He sits up. He shakes his head. He gets
to his feet. He walks unsteadily to the sofa and sits down.*

THE HUSBAND *walks to the suitcase. He stands for some time with a brooding expression.*

THE WIFE. There's no use brooding about it.

THE HUSBAND. About what?

THE WIFE. Being overcharged.

THE HUSBAND. For what?

THE WIFE. *Indicating* THE INFANT. Him.

THE HUSBAND. Oh, that. . . . I wasn't overcharged. . . . I only paid him half what I owed him. . . . I paid him with counterfeit Confederate money. . . . I didn't pay him.

THE HUSBAND *goes to the clothes tree. He takes* THE WIFE's. He goes to THE WIFE *and gives her the coat.* THE WIFE *puts the coat on.* THE HUSBAND *picks up the suitcase, with difficulty.* THE HUSBAND *and* THE WIFE *walk towards the right.*

THE ATTENDANT (AS DOCTOR). Wait, sir! You've forgotten something.

THE HUSBAND *and* THE WIFE *halt and face* THE ATTENDANT (AS DOCTOR).

THE ATTENDANT (AS DOCTOR) *points to* THE INFANT. That is what I mean, sir.

THE HUSBAND *looks at* THE INFANT *quizzically.* That? . . . What is it?

THE ATTENDANT (AS DOCTOR) It's an infant, sir. It's a son.

THE HUSBAND. A Sun?

THE ATTENDANT (AS DOCTOR). Yes. You have a son.

THE HUSBAND. I have a Sun? Impossible. I'm not Chinese.

THE ATTENDANT (AS DOCTOR). *Exasperated.* No, no, no, it's not Chinese.

THE HUSBAND. Japanese?

THE ATTENDANT (AS DOCTOR). No, no, no, it's American.

THE HUSBAND. *Emphatically.* Good. It's a great thing to be an American.

THE ATTENDANT (AS DOCTOR). Indeed. So if you will just take this little patriot . . .

THE HUSBAND. *Emphatically.* It's not a patriot. It has never pledged allegiance to the flag of the United States and to the republic for which it stands.

THE ATTENDANT (AS DOCTOR). No, sir. Take it. You can't leave it here.

THE HUSBAND. Why not?

THE ATTENDANT (AS DOCTOR). The company won't stand the expense, sir. Of the maintenance—or the disposal.

THE HUSBAND *shrugs his shoulders.* Sell it.

THE ATTENDANT (AS DOCTOR). It's not worth anything, sir. . . . No, sir,
   you'll have to take it with you now.
THE HUSBAND. I don't need it.
THE ATTENDANT (AS DOCTOR). No, sir, you can't leave it here for *that*
   reason.
THE HUSBAND. What if I said I don't like it?
THE ATTENDANT (AS DOCTOR) *shakes his head.* Insufficient excuse, sir.
THE HUSBAND. What if I said I have too many of them already? THE
   ATTENDANT (AS DOCTOR) *shakes his head in reply to each question:* It's lazy?
   . . . The neighbors would complain? . . . I don't have a license for it? . . .
   It talks too much? . . . I'm allergic to it? . . . *He shrugs his shoulders.* I really
   don't know what more I could say. . . *As if he thinks of something.* What if I
   said it's a *Marxist?* THE ATTENDANT (AS DOCTOR) continues shaking his
   head. *With increasing desperation,* What if I said it's a *bolshevik? What if I said
   it's a STALINIST?*
THE ATTENDANT (AS DOCTOR). No, sir. I'm afraid you'll have to take it with
   you.
THE HUSBAND. I'll just leave it here for now. I'll have you deliver it. I know
   you deliver.
THE ATTENDANT (AS DOCTOR). Not in that sense of the word, sir. You'll
   have to remove it now.
THE HUSBAND. What's the rush?
THE ATTENDANT (AS DOCTOR). Time is money, sir.
THE HUSBAND. *Suspiciously.* I bet you're trying to get rid of us so you can
   hurry and rent our room to somebody else.
THE ATTENDANT (AS DOCTOR). That's an odds-on bet, sir.
THE HUSBAND. Some people haven't got any courtesy.
THE ATTENDANT (AS DOCTOR). You're platitudinizing, sir .
THE HUSBAND. *Abruptly outraged.* The hell I'm platitudinizing! I have *never*
   platitudized! You'll *never* catch me platitudinizing! *Abruptly calm.* It's *illegal,*
   isn't it?
THE WIFE *tugs at his sleeve and whispers for a few seconds in his ear.*
THE HUSBAND. *To* THE WIFE. That's what *you* say. What can a woman know
   about platitudinizing? *To* THE ATTENDANT (AS DOCTOR). Firmly. I'll let

117

you off this time, buster. Next time it might be a different story. You can just consider yourself lucky. You don't know how close you came just now to being beaten to a bloody pulp.

THE ATTENDANT (AS DOCTOR). *Sarcastic.* I feel very fortunate, sir.

THE WIFE. *Politely.* Good-by.

THE ATTENDANT (AS DOCTOR). *With exaggerated courtesy.* And good-by to *you*, ma'am. *He bows and smiles.* Thank you very much for your patronage. It was my pleasure doing business to you. . . . Until next time, then.

THE HUSBAND. *Positive.* There isn't going to be any next time. We're never coming here again, let me tell you. And you can be damn sure about that.

THE ATTENDANT (AS DOCTOR). Don't be bitter, sir. *He pauses briefly.* Be *sweet.* *He pauses briefly.* Sir, as doctor—that is, as an unchallengeable authority figure, I say incontrovertibly that in life, as in Hollywood, sweetness—*sweetness,* not bitterness—always wins out. *He pauses and smiles, as if proud of himself, and looks around as if daring anyone to contradict him.*

Now then, where were we? . . .

THE HUSBAND. I said I won't ever be back at this place and you begged me to please reconsider.

THE ATTENDANT (AS DOCTOR). *Flatly.* You'll be back, sir.

THE HUSBAND. *Aggressive.* What makes you so sure?

THE ATTENDANT (AS DOCTOR). *Assured.* Our facilities and services being in short supply, the demand for them being great, men being what they are, you being what you are.

THE HUSBAND. *Angry.* Are you trying to *insult* me?

THE ATTENDANT (AS DOCTOR) *smiles broadly.*

THE HUSBAND *glares at* THE ATTENDANT (AS DOCTOR) *and turns away from him. He picks up the suitcase, with difficulty.* THE HUSBAND *and* THE WIFE *walk slowly toward the right.* THE WIFE *draws* THE INFANT *after her.*

THE ATTENDANT (AS DOCTOR) *waves at them. Saccharine.* Good-*by!*

THE HUSBAND *and* THE WIFE *halt. They turn to look at him. He continues to wave.*

THE ATTENDANT (AS DOCTOR). *In the same tone.* Good-*by!*

THE HUSBAND. *Bitter.* Good-by and good riddance. I'll never see his ugly face again. . . . *He abruptly becomes violently angry. He drops the suitcase. The very loud sound-effects thud sounds. Shouting with increasing vehemence.* And when I see his ugly face again I'm going to crack his skull! . . . I'm going to tear him limb from 939limb! . . . I'm going to tear him into a million pieces! . . . I'm going to annihilate his atoms! . . . . I'm going to explode his notions!

THE WIFE. *Calmly.* Get the bag.

THE HUSBAND. *Abruptly calm.* What?

THE WIFE. *Annoyed, weary.* Come on. Let's go. Get the bag.

THE HUSBAND *looks around as if he did not see the bag.* What bag? *He picks up the bag.* THE HUSBAND *and* THE WIFE *walk to the right.* THE INFANT *runs to catch up with them.* THE WIFE *takes his hand and draws him after her.*

THE ATTENDANT (AS DOCTOR) *waves at them again. In the same saccharine voice.* Good-by!

THE ATTENDANT (AS DOCTOR) *takes the money from the pocket of his jacket and puts it in his wallet. He faces* THE DIRECTOR *and raises the wallet as a priest raises the Host.* Blessèd Bread. . . . So nutritious to the spirit. *He pauses.* Of cupidity. *He pauses, apparently thinking profoundly.* God is . . . is—*He pauses, trying to think of what he is going to say next; suddenly it occurs to him. Firmly.*—a capitalist. *There is a pause while he considers matters.* And for us all all is well. *He pauses again, reconsiders.* Well, as well as can be expected. *Pauses, considering further.* Under the circumstances. *He puts the wallet in the left inside breast pocket of his jacket. He crosses his hands on the jacket over the pocket and his heart. There is a pause. He face is expressionless. He drops his hands and walks offstage to the right.*

THE DIRECTOR *closes the script. He takes the record from the turntable and puts it in its sleeve. He takes the script and record and stands up. He points to the lights with the baton and makes a downward pumping motion, signaling for the lights to go down. He climbs down the ladder and the lights go down as he reaches the floor.*

Made in the USA
Middletown, DE
20 April 2021